The
People's
Bible

ROLAND CAP EHLKE
General Editor

ARMIN J. PANNING
New Testament Editor

MENTOR KUJATH
Manuscript Editor

Mark

HAROLD E. WICKE

NORTHWESTERN PUBLISHING HOUSE
Milwaukee, Wisconsin

The cover and interior illustrations are from the originals by James
Tissot (1836-1902). The map of Paul's journey was drawn by Dr. John
Lawrenz. The map of Palestine in the time of Christ was drawn by
Harold Schmitz.

Scripture taken from the
HOLY BIBLE, NEW INTERNATIONAL VERSION.
Copyright © 1973, 1978, 1984 International Bible Society.
Used by permission of Zondervan Bible Publishers.

Library of Congress Card 87-61757
Northwestern Publishing House
1250 N. 113th St., P.O. Box 26975, Milwaukee, WI 53226-0975
© 1988 by Northwestern Publishing House.
Published 1988
Printed in the United States of America
ISBN 0-8100-0271-X

CONTENTS

ILLUSTRATIONS

EDITOR'S PREFACE

The People's Bible is just what the name implies — a Bible for the people. It includes the complete text of the Holy Scriptures in the popular New International Version. The commentary following the Scripture sections contains personal applications as well as historical background and explanations of the text.

The authors of *The People's Bible* are men of scholarship and practical insight, gained from years of experience in the teaching and preaching ministries. They have tried to avoid the technical jargon which limits so many commentary series to professional Bible scholars.

The most important feature of these books is that they are Christ-centered. Speaking of the Old Testament Scriptures, Jesus himself declared, "These are the Scriptures that testify about me" (John 5:39). Each volume of *The People's Bible* directs our attention to Jesus Christ. He is the center of the entire Bible. He is our only Savior.

The commentaries also have maps, illustrations and archaeological information when appropriate. All the books include running heads to direct the reader to the passage he is looking for.

This commentary series was initiated by the Commission on Christian Literature of the Wisconsin Evangelical Lutheran Synod.

It is our prayer that this endeavor may continue as it began. We dedicate these volumes to the glory of God and to the good of his people.

Roland Cap Ehlke

INTRODUCTION

The New Testament opens with four Gospels — Matthew, Mark, Luke and John. None of the Gospels state the names of their authors. However that does not mean they are anonymous. The early church in whose midst the Gospels were written and to whom they were originally addressed testifies as to their authors. We have no reason to doubt its testimony.

The church historian Eusebius, who lived A.D. 275-339, in his *Ecclesiastical History* quotes from a lost book of the church father Papias (A.D. 140). In this quotation Papias cites John the Apostle calling him the Elder, the very term by which John speaks of himself in 2 and 3 John. The quotation in Eusebius reads: "The Elder said this also: Mark, who became Peter's interpreter, wrote accurately, though not in order, all that he remembered of the things said or done by the Lord. For he had neither heard the Lord nor been one of his followers, but afterwards, as I said, he had followed Peter, who used to compose his discourses with a view to the needs of his hearers, but not as though he were drawing up a connected account of the Lord's sayings. So Mark made no mistake in thus recording some things just as he remembered them. For he was careful of this one thing, to omit none of the things he had heard and to make no untrue statements therein." Thus the apostolic authority of Peter as well as the apostolic authority of John support the Gospel of Mark, not to mention the authority of Paul (see 2 Timothy 4:11).

More than that. Mark's Gospel was also written by inspiration and thus contains what God the Holy Spirit wanted the church to know, both the first readers and its present readers, including you and me. Though Paul was specifically speaking of the Old Testament when he wrote the words of 2 Timothy 3:16,17: "All Scripture is God-breathed and is useful for teaching, rebuking, correcting and training in righteousness, so that the man of God may be thoroughly equipped for every good work," yet these words also apply to everything recorded in the New Testament, including the Gospel of Mark.

Why did the Holy Spirit give us four Gospels in the New Testament? Though there is much repetition of material in them, yet all four have their own way of applying it and their own reason for including it. A comparison of what they have in common shows no distortion or amending of facts. The Gospel writers were chosen and moved by the Spirit of God to record the gospel according to their own special abilities and interests, thus to meet your needs and mine, though we too are all different.

Matthew is clearly interested in presenting Christ as the fulfillment of Old Testament prophecy. His Gospel would therefore have been of special interest to those who came to Christ among Israel. Luke's purpose meets the needs of a man named Theophilus, seemingly a recent convert who needed to be "assured." Luke therefore goes into great detail, particularly concerning the early years of our Lord's life. Furthermore, what Luke wrote was also based on thorough personal investigation that included interviewing eyewitnesses and researching previously written records of our Lord's life now no longer in existence, unless the Gospels of Matthew and Mark are included among them. John, the last of the Gospels, written shortly before A.D. 100, supplements the earlier Gospels where necessary and reveals a decidedly theological trend particularly dealing with our Lord's deity and his relationship to the Father and the Holy Spirit. Over one-half of John's Gospel deals with Christ's words and acts during his last days here on earth.

By contrast Mark, the shortest of the Gospels, deals in greater detail with our Lord's acts than with his sayings. Mark as author quotes the Old Testament only once and that in his opening statement. It is clear he wrote for an audience who had indeed heard the gospel message but was not intimately acquainted with the Old Testament. His was undoubtedly a predominantly Gentile readership, for he makes it a point to translate all Aramaic expressions and to explain Hebrew customs, something that would not have been necessary had the majority of his readers grown up in the synagogue. That he also uses numerous Latin words and expressions suggests his first readers undoubtedly were Romans or were from Italy.

When reading John's Gospel one must pause and reflect at almost every sentence. Not so with Mark. His is a book of action that rapidly proceeds from one incident to another. It pictures our Lord's active ministry as he helps men and women in their distress and then in his passion carries out God's good and gracious will to save us. Jesus is a man among men, but at the same time Mark's narrative opens our eyes to see that this man is at the same time the very Son of God, the Savior of mankind. As our Lord step-by-step teaches his disciples through word and deed to recognize who he truly is, we too are supported in our faith to say with Peter, "You are the Christ" (Mark 8:29) and with the centurion standing beneath the cross, "Surely this man was the Son of God!" (Mark 15:39). Jesus having arisen and ascended into heaven, we too are moved by Mark's account to join the disciples of whom it is said, "Then the disciples went out and preached everywhere, and the Lord worked with them" (Mark 16:20).

We see that Mark's Gospel is very practical. It helped the church of his day and helps the church of today to answer mankind's questions about sin and salvation, about Christ and Christian living.

Who is the writer who has given us this account of our Lord's life, death and resurrection that so grips our hearts and makes us ready to follow him? He was a man who himself had to learn step-by-step to follow the Lord about whom he later wrote. We with the early church have identified him as John Mark, the cousin of Barnabas. His Hebrew name was John and his Latin name Mark. We find him referred to in Scripture for the first time in Acts 12:12: "He [Peter] went to the house of Mary the mother of John, also called Mark, where many people had gathered and were praying." His mother was a member of the Christian congregation in Jerusalem which was praying for the release of Peter after he had been arrested and imprisoned by Herod Agrippa. That Peter was released by an angel in answer to prayer must have made a deep impression upon Mark. Whether he himself ever saw Christ is not stated in the Bible, but it is possible (Mark 14:51). We are not told just when he came to faith in Christ as the Savior promised in the Old Testament. However when a few years later his cousin Barnabas and the Apostle Paul were commissioned by the church in Antioch to carry the gospel into Asia Minor, we read that they took John Mark along as one of their helpers (see Acts 13:5). His work certainly wasn't only that of a porter, but must have included giving witness to the gospel.

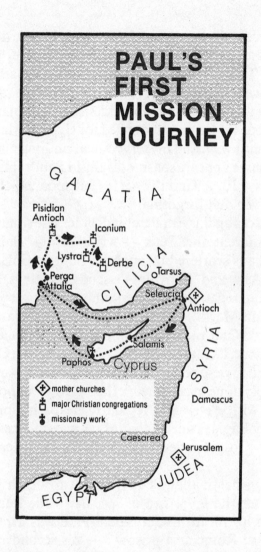

PAUL'S FIRST MISSION JOURNEY

GALATIA

Pisidian Antioch

Iconium

Lystra   Derbe

Tarsus

Perga
Attalia

CILICIA

Seleucia

Antioch

Salamis

Paphos   Cyprus

SYRIA

Damascus

mother churches

major Christian congregations

missionary work

Caesarea

Jerusalem

JUDEA

EGYPT

During this mission journey he heard both Paul and his own cousin proclaim the good news and certainly must have heard all about Paul's conversion on the road to Damascus. Yet at Perga in Pamphilia John Mark left them to return to Jerusalem. Whatever the reason was, and it could not have been an acceptable one, Paul did not trust him sufficiently to take him along on his second missionary journey (see Acts 15:37,38). This led to a rift between Paul and Barnabas, so that each went his own way. It was, we can say in retrospect, the Lord's way of putting more mission teams on the road, for Barnabas took Mark and sailed for Cyprus. Mark had to learn the hard way, and in Acts we hear nothing more about him. His name appears spasmodically in Paul's epistles, e.g., Colossians 4:10; 2 Timothy 4:11; Philemon 24. Paul must have forgiven and forgotten.

He surfaces again with Peter in Rome. The situation is an entirely different one. Peter — writing from "Babylon" to the Christians scattered throughout Pontus, Galatia, Cappadocia, Asia and Bithynia — sends greetings from the Roman congregation and then adds the words: "And so does my son Mark" (1 Peter 5:13). This reveals two things about Mark. One, the relationship between Peter and Mark was very close, like father and son. The other, the Christians in Asia Minor were acquainted with Mark. This suggests he had possibly done mission work there. However now he was in Rome with Peter and regularly heard his preaching. That's why Papias can say that Mark was an interpreter of Peter. His Gospel reflects the preaching and teaching of Peter.

Tradition has it that Peter was put to death in Rome shortly after the great fire of A.D. 64, while Paul was in Spain. On his return to Jerusalem Paul was arrested and sent back to Rome as a prisoner — his second imprisonment. From prison he wrote to Timothy in Asia Minor asking him to hurry to Rome and then added, "Get Mark and bring him with you, because he is helpful to me in my ministry" (2 Timothy 4:11). Whether they reached Rome before Paul was beheaded we do not know. But we do know that Mark had regained the full confidence of this apostle.

What is more, Luke also was with Paul in Rome at that time, so the two Gospel writers who were not themselves apostles had time together and possibly even compared notes. But the latter is conjecture.

Here then is the writer of the second Gospel, a man who had to learn faithfulness the hard way but who then was loved and trusted by the apostles, heard them speak and teach and preach, and was their confidant. What he tells us in his Gospel reflects what he heard from eyewitnesses — from Paul who had seen the Lord by a special revelation after the ascension, from Peter who had walked the highways and byways of Galilee and Judea with Jesus, from Barnabas who was a member of the first Christian congregation in Jerusalem, also from countless other eyewitnesses.

That Mark can rightly be called an interpreter of Peter is evident from all the details and human touches included that only one who had been there could have told Mark. That Mark when mentioning Peter speaks very frankly, not toning down his weaknesses, suggests that by the time Mark wrote his Gospel Peter perhaps was dead but his reputation was a solid one. We thank the Holy Spirit for moving Mark to write thus, for now we who face the same problems can learn from his mistakes and shortcomings and be strengthened in our own faith.

It is a true and living story that Mark records. From his opening words we know that he had a definite purpose in mind. His purpose was not to write a biography, but to present Jesus Christ to us as the man who is the very Son of God sent by the heavenly Father to take our place, that is, to procure salvation for us. Mark's own history shows how God trained him for this task of putting into writing the gospel concerning Christ so that you and I, coming face to face with the Savior in Mark's Gospel, may set our faith on him and live our lives to his glory. Mark opens his Gospel with the words: "The beginning of the gospel about Jesus Christ, the Son of God," to remind his readers — you and me among them — the Savior wants them to be part of the subsequent story. May the Holy Spirit achieve that in our lives through Mark's Gospel!

Since there were no copyright laws back in Mark's day, his Gospel does not give the date when it was made public. From its contents, however, it is clear that it was written some years before the destruction of Jerusalem and at about the time of the Apostle Peter's death or shortly thereafter.

The Gospel About Jesus Christ, the Son of God

PROLOGUE

Title

The first readers of Mark's Gospel undoubtedly were the Christians living in Italy and Rome, for we find Mark in Rome at the close of the Apostle Paul's life (see 2 Timothy 4:11). After the death of the apostles Peter and Paul the people who heard and believed their message would naturally turn to those who had been their assistants and ask them to preach the good news of Jesus Christ in their midst. Soon it also became evident that it would be good and profitable to have their words in writing. In fact, it may have been Peter himself while still among them who suggested this very thing (see 2 Peter 1:12-15). This is the task Mark took upon himself and for which the Holy Spirit chose him even as he called Matthew, Luke and John to similar tasks. Mark opens his Gospel with the following words, words that serve very well as a title for his entire presentation.

1 The beginning of the gospel about Jesus Christ, the Son of God.

Each word of this title is important in order to understand what Mark wishes to transmit to his readers. It is clear that this title is first of all a profound statement of Mark's own faith. Mark is not simply writing a life of Jesus of Nazareth, a biography as it were. He is presenting him to his readers as "Jesus Christ, the Son of God." That's the good news they need to hear. Sinners need a Savior.

The opening words, "the beginning," take all who are acquainted with Scripture back to Genesis 1:1: "In the beginning God created the heavens and the earth." With the coming of Jesus Christ, Mark tells us, there is a new beginning, a new creation. His coming fulfills all the Old Testament promises and prophecies concerning the Savior who would come to redeem men from sin and everlasting death. Mark's words, "the beginning," include everything he wrote in his Gospel. He identifies the new beginning as Jesus Christ and all that he said and did.

As we read these words we naturally also think of their sequel, the story of the gospel's spread throughout the world. A portion of that history is our own coming to faith in Jesus Christ, the Son of God, our Savior. The final chapter of this gospel story will be ushered in on the great day of judgment when the Savior says to us, "Come, you who are blessed by my Father; take your inheritance, the kingdom prepared for you since the creation of the world" (Matthew 25:34).

Mark describes his message as gospel. Gospel means good news. Not all news is good, but that about Jesus Christ, the Son of God, is. The bad news is the news of our sin and its bitter consequences. There was and there is nothing we can do to save ourselves. We desperately need someone to take our place and pay our penalty. That this person came and completely fulfilled all that was promised and foretold Mark designates as the good news. It is thus not at all strange that the word "gospel" was later chosen to designate the four accounts in the New Testament that relate the story of Jesus Christ. Jesus Christ is good news.

The good news which Mark and the other Gospel writers report centers in Jesus of Nazareth. Mark calls him Jesus Christ, the Son of God. Jesus was his personal name chosen by God and revealed to Joseph by the angel saying, "You are to give him the name Jesus, because he will save his people from their sins" (Matthew 1:21). Jesus is the New Testament form of the name Joshua which means "Yahweh is help and salvation." It was a very popular name. But for Jesus of Nazareth it is descriptive of our Lord's mission — to be mankind's Savior.

The name Christ, used here as a proper name, is also descriptive of our Lord's mission. Christ means "the anointed one." This Jesus, of whom Mark writes, is thus not just any Jesus, but the Jesus anointed by the Holy Spirit to be our prophet, priest and king. Jesus himself in his ministry avoided using the name Christ, or Messiah, because by that time the name had been given false, political overtones. He therefore preferred to call himself the Son of Man. Only after he had by word and deed instructed his disciples, did he finally ask them, "Who do you say I am?' and then accept Peter's confession, "You are the Christ" (8:29). And when Caiaphas the high priest asked him, "Are you the Christ, the Son of the Blessed One?" Jesus replied, "I am" (14:61,62).

The emphasis in Mark's opening statement lies on the final words: "The Son of God." This is the point of view from which Mark presents his account of the good news about Jesus Christ. Though Jesus Christ was rejected by his own people and crucified as a malefactor, Mark tells us that he was anything but a malefactor. Mark's answer to the question, "Who is Jesus Christ?" is: He is the man who is the Son of God. The study of Mark's Gospel leads step by step to the conviction arrived at by the centurion at the cross, "Surely this man was the Son of God" (15:39). Jesus Christ of Nazareth, who lived as a man among men, who became tired and hungry and thirsty, who experienced pain and death, was more than just a great man, an eloquent teacher, a mighty miracle worker — he is God the Son, God together with the Father and the Holy Spirit. It is Mark's God-given purpose to lead you and me to recognize the man Jesus Christ as the very Son of God and to confess him as such (see 1:11; 3:11; 5:7; 9:7; 12:16; 13:32; 14:36,61; 15:39). In this Matthew (1:23), Luke (1:35) and John (1:14; 20:31) fully agree with him.

Jesus' Credentials

Verses 2-13 present the credentials of Jesus Christ, the Son of God. His entrance on the scene is prepared by the messenger foretold in the Old Testament. He is approved by the heavenly Father and attested by the Holy Spirit at his baptism. In the temptation that follows he overcomes the archfoe of God and man, Satan.

John the Baptist Prepares the Way

²It is written in Isaiah the prophet: "I will send my messenger ahead of you, who will prepare your way — ³a voice of one calling in the desert, 'Prepare the way for the Lord, make straight paths for him.' "⁴And so John came, baptizing in the desert region and preaching a baptism of repentance for the forgiveness of sins. ⁵The whole Judean countryside and all the people of Jerusalem went out to him. Confessing their sins, they were baptized by him in the Jordan River. ⁶John wore clothing made of camel's hair, with a leather belt around his waist, and he ate locusts and wild honey. ⁷And this was his message: "After me will come one more powerful than I, the thongs of whose sandals I am not worthy to stoop down and untie. ⁸I baptize you with water, but he will baptize you with the Holy Spirit."
(Matthew 3:1-6,11; Luke 3:1-6,16; John 1:15-28)

In the Gospel of Matthew one statement stands out because of constant repetition, the words: "This was to fulfill what was spoken through the prophet. . . . " Matthew stressed that fact because he wrote his Gospel for Jewish readers well-acquainted with the Old Testament. Mark wrote for Gentile readers and so, except for this one instance, does not personally refer to the Old Testament prophecies. In writing his Gospel he simply wants us to observe Jesus in action and in doing so wants us to come to the same conclusion Matthew drew from the Old Testament prophecies he quotes so frequently. The Holy Spirit has blessed both ways of writing, and both are important.

Mark opens his Gospel with the Old Testament prophecy concerning John the Baptist. In thus presenting John's credentials Mark likewise presents the credentials of Jesus Christ, the Son of God, whose forerunner John was. Note, therefore, that Christianity is not a new religion, but is the fulfillment of God's Old Testament promises.

The words Mark quotes are taken from Malachi 3:1 and Isaiah 40:3. Mark mentions only Isaiah because Isaiah was the prophet who spoke about the coming Savior in greater detail than any other Old Testament prophet. It is his words that cause us to understand the words of Malachi, the last of the Old Testament prophets, in their messianic sense. This is therefore not an error on the part of Mark as some commentators insist. It is the Holy Spirit who caused Mark to write as he did. And it is the Holy Spirit who here teaches us that the words of Isaiah, first fulfilled in the return of Israel from Babylon in the days of Cyrus, found their greater fulfillment in John and Jesus.

These Old Testament prophecies make clear it was God who sent John the Baptist as his messenger to announce the coming of his Son and thus to prepare the hearts of his people to receive him. Mark shows us how John fulfilled these words of prophecy. When John the Baptist came, those who saw and heard him could draw only one conclusion, namely, that with the appearance of John the promised Messiah would also soon appear. Comparing prophecy and fulfillment, we have no doubts that he who followed John the Baptist was indeed the promised Messiah. John was God's messenger, God's voice. He did not proclaim his own wisdom, but God's wisdom.

John the Baptist wore rough clothing, woven of camel's hair. His diet was wilderness fare, locusts and wild honey. He was another Elijah, whom 2 Kings 1:8 describes as "a man with a garment of hair and with a leather belt around his waist." When John began his work in the desert region, the uninhabited area near the Jordan, the similarity was not lost on the whole Judean countryside and all the people of Jerusalem who came out to hear him. The twenty-mile journey was an arduous one, downhill from Jerusalem and uphill on the way back. But it took them away from their business deals and their hours of relaxation. They came because they sensed the power of God in John. They were excited. After all, it had been 400 years since a legitimate prophet had appeared on the scene. They had to find out, and they did.

John the Baptist "came, baptizing in the desert region and preaching a baptism of repentance for the forgiveness of sins." Why? Because the hearts of the people had become a desert region, and they needed to be rescued. What he offered them in this baptism of repentance was not merely a ritual washing, but the gift of forgiveness. His baptism was essentially no different from the baptism by which our Lord comes to us today with his pardon and peace. The forgiveness granted through John's baptism was not a reward because they had repented, but a wonderful gift of God who through John's preaching brought them to repentance and gave them a change of heart.

That's why Mark does not emphasize John's preaching of the law, although John did that too as is evident from the other Gospels. John the Baptist's message, as recorded by Mark, was the gospel pointing forward to Jesus Christ and his great work of redemption. John did not claim to be what

14

he was not. He was not the Christ, and he set the record straight when he said, "After me will come one more powerful than I, the thongs of whose sandals I am not worthy to stoop down and untie." In Jesus' presence John the forerunner did not even consider himself worthy to render the service of a slave.

Note also the comparison: "I baptize you with water, but he will baptize you with the Holy Spirit." Shortly before his ascension into heaven, Jesus explained John's words. In Acts 1:5 Jesus said, "For John baptized with water, but in a few days you will be baptized with the Holy Spirit." Thus the words of John referred to the day of Pentecost, when the church was indeed to experience the power of the Holy Spirit. In the months before, people had turned away from Christ. On Pentecost after Peter proclaimed Christ, we read: "Those who accepted his message were baptized, and about three thousand were added to their number that day" (Acts 2:41).

But all this depended on something else, something that had to precede, and that is our Lord's work of redemption. It is only because of that, that John's baptism brought forgiveness of sins and that God today deals with us in the same way in Word and sacrament. Without Christ this could never be accomplished. That's why John was sent — to prepare the people to receive Christ. His coming assures us this Jesus Christ, the Son of God, is our Savior. John is and remains one of Jesus' credentials. John the Baptist is part of the beginning of the gospel about Jesus Christ, the Son of God.

The Baptism of Jesus

[9]At that time Jesus came from Nazareth in Galilee and was baptized by John in the Jordan. [10]As Jesus was coming up out of the water, he saw heaven being torn open and the Spirit descend-

15

ing on him like a dove. ¹¹And a voice came from heaven: "You are my Son, whom I love; with you I am well pleased."
(Matthew 3:13-17; Luke 3:21,22; John 1:32)

Mark, in telling of the baptism of Jesus with the subsequent bestowal of the Holy Spirit and the Father's commendation, offers a second credential to assure us Jesus of Nazareth is indeed "Jesus Christ, the Son of God." Note that Scripture nowhere prescribes the mode of baptism — whether by immersion, pouring or sprinkling. Rather, it concerns itself with what God does for us through baptism.

John the Baptist's activity and proclamation were a sign to Jesus that the hour had come for him to enter upon his redemptive work. Thus he left Nazareth and came to John at the Jordan River without being compelled or summoned. He asked John to baptize him and thus to inaugurate him into his office. As we know from the Gospel of Matthew, the baptism of Jesus presented a problem for John, for Jesus did not need "a baptism of repentance for the forgiveness of sins." Jesus assured John that it was proper for him to be baptized and for John to perform the baptism "to fulfill all righteousness." It was John's obligation as God's messenger and Jesus' obligation as the Promised One to inaugurate God's plan of salvation. By insisting on being baptized, Jesus deliberately took our place as God the Father had sent him to do. "God made him who had no sin to be sin for us, so that in him we might become the righteousness of God" (2 Corinthians 5:21). Officially the work of redemption began here and was completed on Calvary.

When Jesus stepped on shore after being baptized by John, God himself gave his sanction and approval to Jesus' action. First of all, the heavens opened and the Spirit of God descended on Jesus in the form of a dove. The dove was a symbol of sacrifice. This was not just a vision granted to

Jesus, but was seen by John and the bystanders, for in John 1:32 John the Baptist testifies he saw the Spirit descend on Jesus. What was the purpose and why was this necessary? The purpose we learn in Acts 10:38: "God anointed Jesus of Nazareth with the Holy Spirit and power." With this God publicly set him apart for his great task. At the same time, with the Spirit at his side, he was also empowered to carry out that task. This was necessary, for we read in Philippians 2:7,8 that Christ Jesus "made himself nothing, taking the very nature of a servant, being made in human likeness. And being found in appearance as a man, he humbled himself and became obedient to death — even death on a cross!"

This explains much of his agony in Gethsemane and lets us understand how he was able to overcome though a true human being, our substitute. Here the coming of the Holy Spirit on him is also the Spirit's designation that this human being is indeed the promised Savior, the Son of God.

Then came the Father's voice from heaven. The Father clearly identified Jesus as his Son. With the word "love" he did not express a sentimental attachment, but expressed his complete approval of what Jesus was undertaking for the descendants of Adam and Eve. The Father also expressed his complete confidence in Jesus by saying, "With you I am well pleased." He publicly acknowledged he had not made a mistake in assigning this task to Jesus. God thereby also acknowledged that Jesus' previous life — in Bethlehem, Egypt and Nazareth — had been without fault. He had not become guilty of the mortal error into which Adam and Eve had fallen. Thus Christ's credentials were perfect. We are to know that, even as Jesus himself was assured of that at his baptism.

Before we consider the third credential Mark brings, we want to note that God at the baptism of Jesus is clearly revealed as three persons — the Father speaking from heaven, the Son standing on the shore of the Jordan, the Holy Spirit descending from the opened heaven. Neither John the Baptist nor others present raise any questions about that. Though the Old Testament clearly states, "The Lord our God, the Lord is one," it also reveals that there are three persons in the Godhead. Those who reject that teaching of the Old Testament Scripture reject it because they reject Christ. How God is one and at the same time three is not revealed. But the truth is revealed so that we may without hesitation believe that Jesus Christ, our Savior and Redeemer, is God the Son.

The Temptation of Jesus

12 At once the Spirit sent him out into the desert, 13and he was in the desert forty days, being tempted by Satan. He was with the wild animals, and angels attended him.
(Matthew 4:1-11; Luke 4:1-13)

Immediately the Spirit sent Jesus into the desert for his first encounter with Satan, the devil who had caused Adam and Eve to fall into sin and thus bring sin upon the entire human race. Jesus faced him alone; no fellow believers were present to comfort and strengthen him. Wild animals were no source of spiritual help. Jesus had to face this battle alone. He was fighting this battle as the substitute for all humans.

The battle was arduous and long. It lasted forty days with no breathing spells — totally unlike the forty days Moses had spent on the mountain with God (see Exodus 24:18), totally different from the forty days Elijah spent on the way to Horeb sustained by the food God had provided (see 1 Kings 19:8). For Jesus they were forty days of continuous testing. Matthew and Luke relate three specific attacks of Satan; Mark simply presents the antagonists, Jesus and Satan.

Do not think this battle was relatively simple for Jesus because he could not possibly sin. As a man he could suffer hunger and thirst, appreciate power and wealth, and thus he felt the pressures of these temptations. Nor was it simple for him because he was the Son of God. Though Jesus during his ministry often used his almighty power to heal and to bless, he seldom used it to defend himself. He faced temptation in the same way you and I must face it — with the Word of God. This was also not the only time Jesus had to face the devil. Jesus continued to fight him until the moment on the cross when he said, "It is finished!"

When he had won the battle in the wilderness, Jesus was completely exhausted. It is then that "angels attended him." Noting this, we are moved to pray as Luther did in his morning and evening prayers: "Let your holy angel be with me, so that the devil may have no power over me."

Our Lord leaves the battlefield qualified to meet every challenger and every challenge. His credentials are perfect: he is acknowledged by the promised forerunner; he is accepted by the Father and blessed by the Spirit; he meets and defeats Satan. Thus he enters on his ministry. In reading the Gospel of Mark we observe his deeds, hear his words and learn to rejoice in "the beginning of the gospel about Jesus Christ, the Son of God."

JESUS REVEALED AS THE CHRIST, THE SON OF GOD, IN HIS MINISTRY IN GALILEE AND THE REGIONS BEYOND

Jesus' Early Galilean Ministry
JESUS BEGINS HIS MINISTRY IN GALILEE
Calling of the First Disciples

¹⁴After John was put in prison, Jesus went into Galilee, proclaiming the good news of God. ¹⁵"The time has come," he said. "The kingdom of God is near. Repent and believe the good news!"
¹⁶As Jesus walked beside the Sea of Galilee, he saw Simon and his brother Andrew casting a net into the lake, for they were fishermen. ¹⁷"Come, follow me," Jesus said, "and I will make you fishers of men." ¹⁸At once they left their nets and followed him.
¹⁹When he had gone a little farther, he saw James son of Zebedee and his brother John in a boat, preparing their nets. ²⁰Without delay he called them, and they left their father Zebedee in the boat with the hired men and followed him.
(Matthew 4:12,17-22; Luke 5:1-11)

Mark's account of the ministry of Jesus begins with the imprisonment of John the Baptist. It is difficult to determine exactly how long this was after the baptism of Jesus and his testing in the wilderness, perhaps as much as half a year. John in his Gospel records some of the events that took place during this time.

When Jesus returned from the wilderness, John was still preaching and baptizing in Bethany on the other side of the

20

Jordan (thus distinguished from Bethany near Jerusalem, the hometown of Mary, Martha and Lazarus). John's message had not changed; he was still proclaiming Christ Jesus as the Lamb of God, who takes away the sin of the world. So it was not at all surprising that he urged some of his own disciples, among them John and Andrew, Peter and Philip, to follow Christ. Mark's account of the calling of Peter, Andrew, James and John therefore does not mark the first time they met Jesus nor the beginning of Jesus' ministry. Jesus had already spent time proclaiming his message in Jerusalem, Judea, Samaria and in parts of Galilee. Sometimes the disciples accompanied him and sometimes not. In fact, Jesus' disciples were not restricted to the Twelve. In Luke 10:1 seventy-two were sent out on a preaching journey by our Lord. When in Galilee, many of them spent part of their time at home, following their occupations. Galilee was home for most of them and also for the majority of the first Christians. Galilee, even though also under the control of Herod who imprisoned John the Baptist, was nevertheless very open to non-Jewish influence. When opposition surfaced in Jerusalem, Jesus moved the thrust of his ministry to Galilee. Much remained to be done and to be taught before the disciples would be prepared for Jesus' passion.

Mark summarizes the message Christ proclaimed. It was "the good news of God," or, in Christ's own words, "The time has come. The kingdom of God is near. Repent and believe the good news (gospel)." This message led its first hearers back into the Scripture which they had heard in their synagogues and which some of them did understand in its proper religious sense. Already at the presentation of the infant Jesus in the temple we become aware of that. Simeon is described as "waiting for the consolation of Israel," and Anna "spoke about the child to all who were looking forward to the redemption of Jerusalem." Their faith was based on

21

the Old Testament promises of the Savior, like Deuteronomy 18:15: "The Lord your God will raise up for you a prophet like me from among your own brothers," and Jeremiah 23:5,6: " 'The days are coming,' declares the Lord, 'when I will raise up to David a righteous Branch, a King who will reign wisely and do what is just and right in the land. In his days Judah will be saved and Israel will live in safety. This is the name by which he will be called: The Lord Our Righteousness.' " So when Jesus now proclaimed, "The time has come. The kingdom of God is near," those who knew their Old Testament and did not misinterpret it politically were quickened in their hearts and looked for the King.

The way to the King, as Christ points out, is to "repent and believe the good news." Repent means to have a change of heart as far as sin is concerned and in this connection points to the good news concerning the one in whom they would find forgiveness of sins. Jesus called on his hearers to turn away from the service of sin, to be sorry they had fallen away from God, and by faith to trust in him who alone offers forgiveness. Surely that is the good news mankind needs, whether in Galilee or in our own home towns.

With John imprisoned and soon to be executed, Jesus realized that the climax of his own life's work was approaching. It was months later that he revealed this fact to his apostles, but he was aware of it now. He also knew that, when his work of redemption would be complete, he would return to the Father in heaven. So one of the tasks facing him was to choose and instruct a corps of followers who would then become his "witnesses in Jerusalem, and in all Judea and Samaria, and to the ends of the earth" (Acts 1:8). This was the point at which Mark began his account of Jesus' ministry.

To Simon and Andrew, Jesus said, "Come, follow me." He had used the same words before when he asked Philip to follow him, and he would use them again. But here Jesus connected with them a definite promise and planned purpose: "Follow me, and I will make you fishers of men." He was singling them out for the great work of being his chosen apostles. Their number was complete by the time we read Mark 3:13-19. Jesus' final gift in preparing them for their assignment would be the pouring out of the Holy Spirit on Pentecost. In the meantime, though they knew what it meant to be fishermen, they had to learn what it meant to be fishers of men. As we read Mark and the other Gospels, we realize there was no better teacher than Jesus.

The response of Simon, Andrew, James and John was immediate. When Jesus called, they were ready to follow him, for they had learned to love him and believe in him. Business, wealth, family — all were secondary to following Jesus and becoming fishers of men. The same faith that filled their hearts should also fill ours, whether we are pastors, teachers, missionaries or lay Christians. Christ must be first in our lives. Note also that father Zebedee did not object. Without a doubt he together with the hired men continued to bring great sacrifices to support Jesus' mission and the training of his disciples.

Of the disciples named here, Peter (Simon) is mentioned first. From the start he became the spokesman of the apostolic group. The picturesque details in this account and elsewhere in Mark, details that could come only from Peter, demonstrate that Peter was the personal source on whom Mark drew in writing his Gospel. The contact between Peter and Mark was a close one. At the close of his First Epistle, Peter sent greetings to the Christians in Pontus, Galatia, Cappadocia, Asia and Bithynia from "my son Mark."

Jesus Drives Out an Evil Spirit

²¹They went to Capernaum, and when the Sabbath came, Jesus went into the synagogue and began to teach. ²²The people were amazed at his teaching, because he taught them as one who has authority, not as the teachers of the law. ²³Just then a man in their synagogue who was possessed by an evil spirit cried out, ²⁴"What do you want with us, Jesus of Nazareth? Have you come to destroy us? I know who you are — the Holy One of God!"

²⁵"Be quiet!" said Jesus sternly. "Come out of him!" ²⁶The evil spirit shook the man violently and came out of him with a shriek.

²⁷The people were all so amazed that they asked each other, "What is this? A new teaching — and with authority! He even gives orders to evil spirits and they obey him." ²⁸News about him spread quickly over the whole region of Galilee.

(Luke 4:31-37)

John in his Gospel tells us that after performing his first miracle in Cana of Galilee Jesus together with his mother and brothers moved to Capernaum. Its situation on the shore of the Sea of Galilee and at the intersection of several important trade routes made Capernaum an ideal base for carrying the gospel into the regions of Galilee and beyond. Besides, Capernaum was also the home of Zebedee and his sons, James and John, and the home of Peter, whose mother-in-law was living with him.

On the Sabbath following their selection to become fishers of men, Peter, James, John and Andrew together with Jesus attended the synagogue service. Since synagogues had no resident ordained ministers, the rulers of the synagogue would invite some rabbi (teacher) or scribe present to teach the lessons. So it happened that Jesus was often invited to address the congregations.

What Jesus' specific message was on this particular Sabbath Mark does not tell us, but he does tell us about the impression his preaching made on the worshipers. They were amazed, for Jesus did not teach as the teachers of the law did. They always appealed to the interpretations of past rabbis and were particularly adept at breaking down God's word into any number of legalistic regulations. Jesus instead always proclaimed the gospel of God. He quoted no experts, but proclaimed the good news on his own authority. This was one of the first lessons the disciples had to learn, namely, that in Jesus they were face to face with the final authority. For us too Christ is more than just a wise teacher or a model to pattern our lives on. He is the one who in word and deed reveals to us the undeserved love of God for sinners incorporated in his own person. His is the final word.

It is not at all surprising that Satan, despite his defeat in the wilderness, was not ready to let such a message and such a preacher go unchallenged. It is the devil who caused a man in that synagogue to cry out against Jesus, for it is clear that this man was not speaking for himself. He could not of himself have known what he said about Christ. However Satan and the evil spirit which possessed this man knew who Jesus of Nazareth was and what his purpose was. They knew he was the Son of God and that he had come to destroy Satan's hold over mankind. With his words Satan revealed himself wiser than many modern theologians. This knowledge did him no spiritual good; it only filled him with fear and trembling. He knew that he faced hell and the gospel was not meant for him.

Though what the evil spirit said was the truth, Jesus would not accept his words as testimony. Satan was not a proper witness, for those hearing him could say, "Those are the words of the father of lies. How can we believe them?" Besides, Jesus was not as yet ready to proclaim openly that he was the Messiah. Most of his audience would have read political aims into that word (see John 6:15). That's why Jesus told the evil spirit, "Be quiet!"

Our Lord indeed had compassion on the man possessed by the evil spirit — a most dreadful condition, as we see when the spirit left him. "Come out of him!" the Lord commanded, and the evil spirit could not resist. This brought home to the people, including the Lord's disciples, that Jesus spoke with authority. A simple command — no elaborate incantation — and the spirit had to obey. Jesus was and is Lord.

Many theologians deny the possibility of demon-possession then and now. It is true that we today do not identify many such cases. Perhaps the trouble is with us — we fail to recognize them. But we also know that Satan and his evil angels are sufficiently wise to adapt themselves to the times. Today we find their power displayed in the human attempts — usually by highly educated persons — to undermine Scripture and its teachings. False doctrine, cults, pagan religions, science that rejects Scripture — all these are the working of Satan. Since they attack us on all sides, we too need to turn to Christ and to the Scriptures for refuge. Jesus, the holy one of God, points us to the Scriptures and testifies, "Your Word is truth."

News was made that day at Capernaum. It is not surprising to read at the close of this episode: "News about him spread quickly over the whole region of Galilee." This too helped to prepare the way for him and his message. Crowds would soon gather wherever he went.

Jesus Heals Peter's Mother-in-law and Many Others

29 As soon as they left the synagogue, they went with James and John to the home of Simon and Andrew. 30Simon's mother-in-law was in bed with a fever, and they told Jesus about her. 31So he

went to her, took her hand and helped her up. The fever left her and she began to wait on them.

³²That evening after sunset the people brought to Jesus all the sick and demon-possessed. ³³The whole town gathered at the door, ³⁴and Jesus healed many who had various diseases. He also drove out many demons, but he would not let the demons speak because they knew who he was.

(Matthew 8:14-17; Luke 4:38-41)

Jesus and his disciples accepted Peter's dinner invitation and went directly to Peter's home from the synagogue. They had plenty to talk about, but there was to be even more. When they arrived at the house, they found Peter's mother-in-law ill with a fever. The disciples immediately took this matter to Jesus. Was he willing to help them too, or were his miracles meant only to increase his prestige and renown with the multitudes? They immediately experienced that those close to him were also to be recipients of his loving care. Jesus answered their request. The healing was complete and instantaneous. The woman's strength was fully restored. She immediately proceeded to wait on them — her way of expressing her gratitude. Peter never forgot; Mark must have heard it from his lips frequently.

Peter was a married man. Our Lord did not demand celibacy of those called to serve him, not even from the man who became the spokesman of the disciples. Paul in First Corinthians 9:5 states that Peter was not the only one of the apostles who was married, and that even the Lord's brothers were married. What is more, their wives often accompanied the apostles on their missionary journeys. The only thing Jesus required of them is the same he requires of all married couples — faithfulness.

The Sabbath ended at sundown. Immediately a crowd came to the house with their sick and demon-possessed. No matter what the disease, Jesus healed the sick and drove out the demons. Nothing was too difficult for him.

Jesus did not allow the demons to speak. He wanted those who were healed and those who witnessed the healings to draw their own conclusions directly from his words and actions and thus to come to the realization he was more than just a healer of the body; he was the promised Savior from sin.

To apply the blessed lesson of this evening in Capernaum to our own lives, we might read Henry Twells's evening hymn, "At Even, When the Sun Did Set," 557 in *The Lutheran Hymnal.*

Jesus Spends Time in Prayer and Then Leaves on a Tour of Galilee

35Very early in the morning, while it was still dark, Jesus got up, left the house and went off to a solitary place, where he prayed. 36Simon and his companions went to look for him, 37and when they found him, they exclaimed: "Everyone is looking for you!"

38Jesus replied, "Let us go somewhere else — to the nearby villages — so I can preach there also. That is why I have come." 39So he traveled throughout Galilee, preaching in their synagogues and driving out demons.

(Matthew 4:23-25; Luke 4:42-44)

That Sabbath had been an exceptionally busy one for Jesus, yet he did not sleep late the next morning. Instead, he left the house before sunrise and retreated to a solitary place to pray. It may seem strange to us that Jesus the Son of God felt the need to spend time in praying to and communing with his heavenly Father, but only until we remember he was also truly human. As such he too was dependent upon God. However in one respect his prayers were not identical with ours. They were not prayers for the forgiveness of sins, for he had none. In his prayers he talked with his heavenly Father about the work that lay before him and thus found strength for his task. On this particular morning he may well have discussed with the Father whether he should remain longer in Capernaum or begin taking his message into other areas of Galilee. The Father's answer was clear in the words of Jesus to his disciples and in his subsequent action.

That Jesus felt the need for spending time in prayer reminds us that our need to do so is greater. We remember also that the Old Testament prophet Daniel felt the need to kneel in prayer three times a day. Let us take to heart his example and that of our Lord.

Peter and the other disciples had different plans for Jesus. When the crowd gathered again, they discovered that Jesus had left the house. Immediately they began searching for him with Peter leading the search party. That they found him suggests that they were aware of his practice of going apart by himself to pray. They told him about the crowd looking for him. Undoubtedly they thought Jesus would be pleased with that. But Jesus knew many only came to him for what there was in it for them. He also recognized the disciples still had a lot to learn about him and his mission. Had Jesus followed their suggestion, he would not have placed the emphasis on proclaiming the gospel, but on presenting himself as a healer — the error many faith healers are guilty of today.

Jesus therefore informed his disciples on that very morning that he would set out on a preaching tour of Galilee. When Luke (4:44) says "Judea," he is not contradicting Mark, since Judea can also mean "the land of the Jews" (see NIV text note). Wherever Jesus went on this tour, he entered the synagogues. This offered him many opportunities to preach the gospel, since synagogue services were not only conducted on the Sabbath but also on Mondays and Thursdays. In connection with his preaching he also drove out demons, for they were the opponents of his message. The tour may well have lasted several weeks or even months, but Mark summarizes it in one verse. The Savior's emphasis was always on preaching the gospel.

Our Lord saw the need for taking the gospel message beyond Capernaum. That reminds us we too are not to keep the gospel to ourselves, but to share it. In fact, our Lord's last words to his disciples were: "You will be my witnesses in Jerusalem, and in all Judea and Samaria, and to the ends of the earth" (Acts 1:8). That is still our assignment, and in the Gospel of Mark we have our Lord's example.

Jesus Heals a Man Afflicted with Leprosy

⁴⁰A man with leprosy came to him and begged him on his knees, "If you are willing, you can make me clean."

⁴¹Filled with compassion, Jesus reached out his hand and touched the man. "I am willing," he said. "Be clean!" ⁴²Immediately the leprosy left him and he was cured.

⁴³Jesus sent him away at once with a strong warning: ⁴⁴"See that you don't tell this to anyone. But go, show yourself to the priest and offer the sacrifices that Moses commanded for your cleansing, as a testimony to them." ⁴⁵Instead he went out and began to talk freely, spreading the news. As a result, Jesus could no longer enter a town openly but stayed outside in lonely places. Yet the people still came to him from everywhere.

(Matthew 8:2-4; Luke 5:12-16)

The term "leprosy" in Scripture covers a wide variety of skin diseases and is not limited to what today is called Hansen's disease. Whatever form it took, it was contagious, hideous, painful and most often incurable. Those afflicted also became social outcasts. The Levitical law demanded whenever

Healing a Leprous Man

they came near people, they had to cry out, "Unclean, unclean!" Should they ever experience healing, they were required to show themselves to the priests to determine whether they were actually healed or not.

The man who approached Jesus did not cry out, "Unclean," and we can understand why. In his great distress he did not want anyone to stop him from coming to the one he had recognized as being able to do what no one else could do, namely, heal him. Falling on his knees before Jesus —thus expressing his faith that Jesus had divine power and authority to heal and also expressing his own dire need — he cried out, "If you are willing, you can make me clean." He acknowledged Christ's power to heal but did not demand this gift from him. Instead, he cast himself entirely on Christ's mercy. This is how we too are to approach our Lord with our earthly troubles; we are to leave the decision up to him.

Compassion filled Jesus' heart. He did not withhold his blessing. He even ignored that the man had violated the Levitical law by not crying out, "Unclean!" In so doing Jesus indicated when it comes to the requirements of the ceremonial law, love and compassion take precedence over ritual and regulation. Jesus even reached out and touched the man —an act of compassion — although that technically made Jesus himself ceremonially unclean. With one word he cured the leper. He did not have to ask God's permission; he possessed divine authority.

Since Jesus made an exception to the Levitical law, we perhaps are surprised he warned the man not to tell anyone and then ordered him to carry out the other requirements of the Levitical code: "Show yourself to the priest and offer the sacrifices that Moses commanded for your cleansing." (See Leviticus 14). But Jesus himself gave the reason: "as a testimony to them." The priests, we shall see later in Mark's

Gospel, were among Jesus' bitterest opponents, rejecting his deity and his saving mission. However if they had examined this man and pronounced him cured, they would have been unable to deny the divine power of our Lord and unable to deny that one greater than Moses was at work among them.

The reason why Christ did not want the leper to tell others about the miracle becomes clear from what happened when he disobeyed. We must not criticize him for what he did, for if we had been he, we too could not have kept this mighty deed of Christ to ourselves. But the result was Jesus now had to avoid the towns, for the moment he would enter crowds would gather, not to hear his words, but to be cured of their afflictions. Thus what the man did interfered with Jesus' ministry of the word. Even though Jesus avoided towns, people still came to him from everywhere. He was at the height of his popularity. However opposition was about to face him everytime he opened his mouth.

JESUS FACES GROWING OPPOSITION
Jesus Heals a Paralytic

2 **A few days later, when Jesus again entered Capernaum, the people heard that he had come home. ²So many gathered that there was no room left, not even outside the door, and he preached the word to them. ³Some men came, bringing to him a paralytic, carried by four of them. ⁴Since they could not get him to Jesus because of the crowd, they made an opening in the roof above Jesus and, after digging through it, lowered the mat the paralyzed was lying on. ⁵When Jesus saw their faith, he said to the paralytic, "Son, your sins are forgiven."**

⁶Now some teachers of the law were sitting there, thinking to themselves, ⁷"Why does this fellow talk like that? He's blaspheming! Who can forgive sins but God alone?"

⁸Immediately Jesus knew in his spirit that this was what they were thinking in their hearts, and he said to them, "Why are you

thinking these things? ⁹Which is easier: to say to the paralytic, 'Your sins are forgiven,' or to say, 'Get up, take your mat and walk'? ¹⁰But that you may know that the Son of Man has authority on earth to forgive sins. . . . " He said to the paralytic, ¹¹"I tell you, get up, take your mat and go home." ¹²He got up, took his mat and walked out in full view of them all. This amazed everyone and they praised God, saying, "We have never seen anything like this!"

(Matthew 9:1-8; Luke 5:18-26)

After concluding his first preaching tour of Galilee, our Lord returned to his home in Capernaum. He was not granted a prolonged period of rest, for no sooner were people aware that he had come home when so many gathered there that the house was filled and the area around the door jammed. Jesus met their need by preaching the word, just as he had done throughout his tour of Galilee. What set this particular preaching service apart from others was the way Jesus dealt with the paralytic, the answer he gave to the teachers of the law, and that he spoke of himself as the Son of Man.

Palestinian houses were built with flat roofs and outside stairs up to the roofs. The roofs were constructed of tiles and covered with sod. This permitted the friends of the paralytic to dig through the roof and let their friend down directly in front of Jesus. These men were not only ingenious, but they also were persistent. Why? Because they believed Jesus could and would heal their friend. Theirs was a genuine faith in the Lord. And the Lord recognized their actions for what they truly were, acts of faith. Nothing was or is hidden from the Lord.

This becomes even more clear in Jesus' opening words to the paralytic, "Son, your sins are forgiven." Jesus reads the man's heart and knows something infinitely worse than paralysis was troubling him — his sins. Besides, all suffering and disease are really the results of humanity's separation from God. That's why the Lord first meets this need, even as forgiveness is the greatest need of our hearts.

There were some in the audience who did not appreciate this loving word on the part of our Lord. They were the teachers of the law — men who should have known better. They saw in Jesus not God's Son come to redeem them and all men, but a rival who would rob them of the esteem and honor they were accustomed to receive because they were teachers of God's law. Their attitude was inexcusable. They had heard his message and witnessed his miracles, and knowing the Scriptures they had no reason to reject him. But they hardened their hearts. They were present for one purpose alone — to find fault with Jesus. Since our Lord knew this, we are surprised at how gently he dealt with them. He left the door to faith open for them.

The Holy Spirit has Mark record their thoughts and thus reveals to us the condition of their hearts. "Why does this fellow talk like this? He's blaspheming! Who can forgive sins but God alone?" No way were they about to open their hearts to his message. In a contemptuous way they speak of him as "this fellow." They were indeed correct when they said, "Who can forgive sins but God alone?" But they were totally wrong when they said, "He's blaspheming!" God the Father had given them his testimony on the day Jesus was baptized. But they had rejected that testimony and all proof subsequently forthcoming. They remind us of many today, even theologians, who deny that Christ is both divine and human and who reject his resurrection but still want to be members of the church, in fact, its leaders. Human hearts have not changed.

That's why the proof Jesus placed before them is so important today. "Which is easier: to say to the paralytic, 'Your sins are forgiven,' or to say, 'Get up, take your mat and walk' ?" Yes, there is a difference. The teachers of the law would have said, "It's easier for you to say, 'Your sins are forgiven,' because after all we cannot verify it." Actually both are something only God can do, and those to whom God has given the authority and power. To show the teachers of the law how wrong they were, Jesus said to the paralytic, "I tell you, get up, take your mat and go home." He was healed instantly. Note too that Jesus did not say, "I tell you in the name of God," but simply, "I tell you." Jesus' words and actions were telling these teachers, "Open your eyes and hearts. I can do both, forgive and heal. I'm not just 'that fellow'; I am God's Son."

Only Jesus didn't say "Son of God," but "Son of Man." Until the close of his ministry Jesus almost always used this designation in referring to himself. (See 2:28; 8:31,32; 9:9,12,31; 10:33; 13:26; 14:21,41.) He avoided the names Christ and Messiah because the Israel of his day had made them completely political concepts. So Jesus used the name for the coming Savior found in Daniel 7:13,14. It was also used frequently in Ezekiel, but always as the title by which God addressed the prophet himself, never in reference to the coming Savior. In the Gospels Jesus referred to himself as the "Son of Man," that is, the Son of the Most High who had become a human being. He was the Word made flesh.

By using this title our Savior also demonstrated that as the Messiah he was more than just Israel's Savior; he was the Savior of all. The words of Daniel 7:13,14 clearly indicated so: "In my vision at night I looked, and there before me was one like a son of man, coming with the clouds of heaven. He approached the Ancient of Days and was led into his presence. He was given authority, glory and sovereign power; all people, nations and men of every language worshiped him. His dominion is an everlasting dominion that will not pass away, and his kingdom is one that will never be destroyed." That is also how he appears in Revelation 1:12-18 and 14:14. We too shall see him as the Son of Man, our Redeemer, when he comes in the clouds of heaven on the last day.

In contrast to the teachers of the law, the common people at Capernaum that day praised God, saying, "We have never seen anything like this!" Through Mark's account we too are strengthened in our faith in Jesus Christ as the Son of Man, our Savior.

Calls Levi as a Disciple

13Once again Jesus went out beside the lake. A large crowd came to him, and he began to teach them. 14As he walked along, he saw Levi son of Alphaeus sitting at the tax collector's booth. "Follow me," Jesus told him, and Levi got up and followed him.

15While Jesus was having dinner at Levi's house, many tax collectors and "sinners" were eating with him and his disciples, for there were many who followed him. 16When the teachers of the law who were Pharisees saw him eating with the "sinners" and tax collectors, they asked his disciples: "Why does he eat with tax collectors and 'sinners'?"

17On hearing this, Jesus said to them, "It is not the healthy who need a doctor, but the sick. I have not come to call the righteous, but sinners."

(Matthew 9:9-13; Luke 5:27-32)

This is the second in a series of events Mark tells that indicate the growing animosity of the religious leaders of Israel toward Jesus. They made use of every possible opportunity to portray our Lord in a bad light. They continued to do so in the days when Mark wrote his Gospel in order to wean believers away from the truth in Christ. Thus Mark had reason to tell how Jesus had dealt with them. Jesus did not sit back and say nothing. In our day too we must defend the flock against those within and without the visible church who attack and seek to downgrade our Lord and ridicule faith in him. The event recorded here took place as Jesus was proclaiming the word to a large crowd beside the Sea of Galilee.

Jesus came to the tax collector's booth situated on the intersection of several important highways or trade routes running through Capernaum. He invited the tax collector to become one of his disciples. Since we have not met Levi before, it seems rather sudden. It need not be, since we are told by Mark many tax collectors and "sinners" were among those who followed Jesus, those eager to hear his word. The man's name was Levi the son of Alphaeus; his later apostolic name was Matthew (3:18). Undoubtedly he too had heard Christ a number of times and had come to believe and trust in him. At any rate, his decision was immediate — no hesitation whatever. "Levi got up and followed him." And, make no mistake, that was a sacrifice. There was no going back to his job during intervals when Jesus and his disciples were not so busy, as for example Peter, Andrew, James and John with their fishing (1:16-20). His sacrifice was greater than that of the others, but the Holy Spirit honored him in choosing him to be the writer of the Gospel according to Saint Matthew.

As far as the Pharisees were concerned, Jesus' calling a tax collector to be a disciple (and later to be an apostle) was a clear demonstration that Jesus did not take God's law seriously. The teachers of the law looked upon tax collectors as traitors to their race, servants of the hated Herod Antipas and menials of heathen Rome. They were "sinners," outcasts from the synagogue.

The NIV places the word "sinners" here in quotation marks to indicate it is being used in a special sense, a judgmental sense, with judgment passed on them by the Pharisees, not by Christ. In verse 17 Christ uses the same word in its normal sense, applicable to the Pharisees as well as to the tax collectors and to all people.

Undoubtedly some tax collectors were extortioners, but others were not. Levi did not feel compelled to speak as did Zacchaeus, the tax collector at Jericho, who at a dinner given in honor of Christ said, "Look, Lord! Here and now I give half of my possessions to the poor, and if I have cheated anybody out of anything, I will pay back four times the amount" (Luke 19:8).

The Pharisees did not recognize Christ was actually fulfilling the will of God by seeking the lost and welcoming the opportunity of sharing the word of salvation with them. Their ignorance of Christ's purpose also shows their ignorance of the purpose of the law in the Old Testament. Its purpose was not to save people, but to separate them from everything that could cut them off from God and his saving gospel promises. In expounding the law by dissecting it into a multitude of commandments they destroyed both the moral and ceremonial purpose of the law. They thus exposed their legalism and their complete spiritual ignorance of God's purpose in sending Christ, a purpose revealed in the Old Testament.

Their hardness of heart is shown by their question addressed not to Christ, but to the disciples. In this way they wished to raise questions in the hearts of the disciples and thus bring about a breach between them and Christ. That's why Christ himself answered their question. He set them straight and at the same time instructed his disciples.

The answer is logical, theological and gospel-oriented: "It is not the healthy who need a doctor, but the sick. I have not come to call the righteous, but sinners." Thus he tells the disciples and the guests at Levi's house he is indeed the physician whom they need and is ready to meet their needs. And he tells the Pharisees to examine their own hearts. Thus he is also proposing that we ask ourselves: Am I healthy or sick? Am I righteous, or am I a sinner? The self-righteous, like the Pharisees of old, may perhaps at first feel insulted, but the longer they face the question the more uneasy they will become. May this lead us to discover the gospel truth that Jesus is indeed the "Christ, the Son of God," sent to save us.

Jesus Questioned About Fasting

18Now John's disciples and the Pharisees were fasting. Some people came and asked Jesus, "How it is that John's disciples and the disciples of the Pharisees are fasting, but yours are not?"

19Jesus answered, "How can the guests of the bridegroom fast while he is with them? They cannot, so long as they have him with them. 20But the time will come when the bridegroom will be taken from them, and on that day they will fast.

21"No one sews a patch of unshrunk cloth on an old garment. If he does, the new piece will pull away from the old, making the tear worse. 22And no one pours new wine into old wineskins. If he does, the wine will burst the skins, and both the wine and the wineskins will be ruined. No, he pours new wine into new wineskins."

(Matthew 9:14-17; Luke 5:33-39)

It is possible the feast Levi made for Jesus and his disciples and his own friends took place on a day when the Pharisees fasted and thus suggested the question. God in his law had decreed only one day of fasting a year, the great Day of Atonement. After the return from exile the people of Israel, the Old Testament church, had added four more. But the Pharisees insisted all truly religious people ought to fast twice a week, on Monday and Thursday. In the case of all too many their fasting did not come from the heart and thus was of no value whatever. John's disciples' fasting undoubtedly was a mark of grief, for John the Baptist had been imprisoned (1:14). But the contrast was glaring between the followers of the Pharisees and those of John on the one hand, and Jesus and his disciples on the other hand. Naturally the Pharisees, the disciples of John (cf. Matthew 9:14) and others would be led to ask "Why?" But when asked by the Pharisees, the question was a jab at Jesus and suggested he and his disciples were not truly pious, God-fearing children of God.

Jesus' answer put everything into the right perspective. Jesus took up where John the Baptist ended in one of his last public testimonies concerning Christ in John 3:28,29. John said, "You yourselves can testify that I said, 'I am not the Christ but am sent ahead of him.' The bride belongs to the bridegroom. The friend who attends the bridegroom waits and listens for him, and is full of joy when he hears the bridegroom's voice. The joy is mine, and it is now complete." Jesus in effect answered, "I am that bridegroom." Thus it would be improper for his disciples to express sadness by fasting. That would be out of place in the presence of the bridegroom. At the same time Jesus' words were an invitation to join the wedding feast.

Even as John's disciples then were expressing their sorrow by fasting, so there would come a time when Jesus' disciples would also, when the bridegroom would be taken away from them. It is clear that the Lord had full knowledge of what lay ahead, his suffering and death. He also knew how this would affect his disciples. The Gospels record that they fled and that they met only behind closed doors. No feast,

41

only sorrow of which fasting was one outward sign. This is the first time in Mark's Gospel that Jesus spoke about his coming death, and then in very veiled words. There was no suggestion at all he would try to avoid it, for he said, "The time will come." The opposition he was beginning to experience was an indication to him the time was drawing closer.

The other part of Jesus' answer looks beyond the immediate reaction of his disciples. As the bridegroom he is fulfilling all prophecies of the Old Testament concerning the coming Messiah. With his sacrificial death all these prophecies will have been fulfilled. Thereafter the Lord's true followers will need a new garment and new wineskins; the old wineskins are no longer usable. The Old Testament ceremony will therefore be replaced by the New Testament message. Hebrews 10:1 tells us, "The law is only a shadow of the good things that are coming — not the realities themselves." When our Lord died on the cross for the sins of mankind, the curtain in the temple was torn in two; access to God was wide open. No more need for sacrifices and rituals that pointed forward. Christ had fulfilled all that was promised.

In order to emphasize that the new forms could not be combined with the old forms, our Lord used the picture of an old garment patched with a piece of new cloth fresh from the loom. When washed, the patch would shrink and would only tear the hole larger. And that was just as bad as pouring new wine (in the process of fermentation) into an old container made of goatskin that had already been stretched as far as it would go. New wineskins for new wine! Our worship and our forms of service must reflect the fulfillment we have in Christ. Consequently the ceremonial laws of the Old Testament, the old institutions, will have served their purpose. Jesus came to give us a new garment and a new wineskin. And yet, for the moment, Christ and his disciples continued to worship and express their faith according to the forms of the Old Testament dispensation, though not observing the forms added to it by Pharisaism.

The New Testament church in putting these words of Jesus into practice had to face this matter of change repeatedly. The first church convention (see Acts 15) concerned itself with that very matter. Love in seeking not to antagonize those who had come from the synagogue made some decisions. Today with the growth of the church and its complete separation from Judaism the ceremonial laws are no longer being observed. However this does not mean the Old Testament no longer has any importance for us. We value it highly, for it points us to Christ who fulfilled it. In these disputes Christ had with those who questioned and opposed him, Christ prepared the way for our serving him during this New Testament age until he comes again.

Lord of the Sabbath

23One Sabbath Jesus was going through the grainfields, and as his disciples walked along, they began to pick some heads of grain. 24The Pharisees said to him, "Look, why are they doing what is unlawful on the Sabbath?"

25He answered, "Have you never read what David did when he and his companions were hungry and in need? 26In the days of Abiathar the high priest, he entered the house of God and ate the consecrated bread, which is lawful only for priests to eat. And he also gave some to his companions."

27Then he said to them, "The Sabbath was made for man, not man for the Sabbath. 28So the Son of Man is Lord even of the Sabbath."

(Matthew 12:1-8; Luke 6:1-5)

This time the Pharisees were sure they had a case against Jesus. He had not stopped his disciples from picking heads of grain as they were walking through the grainfields on a Sabbath day. It was bad enough when he did not support their fasting principles, but now according to them he was also violating one of God's own Ten Commandments, the one concerning the Sabbath. True, Christ had not done it himself, but his disciples had. What these Pharisees totally ignored was that they themselves had violated the Sabbath by adding hundreds of rules and regulations which were not spelled out in Scripture at all. Thus picking heads of grain to still hunger was in their book equivalent to reaping, threshing, winnowing — all violations of the Sabbath. Outwardly it seemed they had a point, but they had completely misunderstood and misinterpreted not only the Sabbath commandment, but also the rest of the law. They had made it a way of meriting heaven. Pure legalism!

Jesus drew his answer directly from the Scriptures, not from their interpretation of the law. He called attention to what David had done (see 1 Samuel 21). In the holy place of the tabernacle according to God's own instructions there was a golden table with twelve loaves of consecrated bread, one for each of the tribes of Israel. Each Sabbath twelve fresh loaves were offered to God and the old eaten by the priests, but by the priests alone. David, fleeing from the presence of King Saul, appealed to Ahimelech the priest for rations for himself and his band of trusted followers. Since only the "bread of the Presence" was available, Ahimelech gave five of the loaves to David. He recognized that something greater was at stake than just a matter of outward regulations. He was not taken to task for this by God. Jesus in effect said to the Pharisees, "Evidently you haven't really read this Scripture and considered the principle laid down here. Neither David nor Ahimelech as condemned. Human need is of higher consideration to God than religious ritualism."

Then he enunciated clearly the principle that was involved: "The Sabbath was made for man, not man for the Sabbath." It was not created as a means to merit the grace of God, but was God's own gift to man, a day of rest, a day when God would come in a special way to man with his word and a day of worship. The Pharisees had made man a slave to the Sabbath. It was all work-righteousness. This our Lord rejected.

The Sabbath and its regulations were also meant to point Israel forward to the coming Redeemer, and he was now here to fulfill those prophecies. Jesus also told the Pharisees that the Sabbath, originally made for man, also related to him, by saying, "So the Son of Man is Lord even of the Sabbath." Yes, even of the Sabbath, so much more an integral part of God's own Ten Commandments than the matter of fasting on which they had attacked him before. He thus told them what he had permitted his disciples to do on the Sabbath had the full approval of the Father. The Lord of the Sabbath would not permit his disciples to violate the Sabbath. True relationship with God is not of special rules and regulations, but of acceptance of the Son of Man, the Lord of the Sabbath, as the one who has fulfilled all things for us.

Before leaving this section there is a matter that seems like a contradiction between two statements of Scripture. Mark writes that Jesus said, "In the days of Abiathar the priest" (2:26). First Samuel 21:1 reads: "Ahimelech the priest." Actually both of these men were called by both names, sometimes Ahimelech the son of Abiathar and sometimes Abiathar the son of Ahimelech, and sometimes interchangeably. But that's nothing new. Here in chapter 2 Matthew is called Levi, but in 3:19 Levi is called Matthew.

Jesus Heals a Man on the Sabbath

3 **Another time he went into the synagogue, and a man with a shriveled hand was there. ²Some of them were looking for a**

reason to accuse Jesus, so they watched him closely to see if he would heal him on the Sabbath. [3]Jesus said to the man with the shriveled hand, "Stand up in front of everyone."

[4]Then Jesus asked them, "Which is lawful on the Sabbath: to do good or to do evil, to save life or to kill?" But they remained silent.

[5]He looked around at them in anger and, deeply distressed at their stubborn hearts, said to the man, "Stretch out your hand." He stretched it out, and his hand was completely restored. [6]Then the Pharisees went out and began to plot with the Herodians how they might kill Jesus.

(Matthew 12:9-14; Luke 6:6-11)

Despite opposition Jesus continued his ministry of preaching the word. In one of the towns of the area (the name is not given) he entered the synagogue on the Sabbath. As was taking place constantly, the Pharisees had their representatives present to spy on Jesus. This time they thought they would very likely have an airtight case against him. There was a man present at the service whose right hand was shriveled. Would Jesus heal him on the Sabbath? In fact, in Matthew's account they even asked Jesus whether it would be legal to heal on the Sabbath. Jesus answered the question by the example of a sheep fallen into a pit, which all of them would have hauled out. It was indeed lawful to heal on the Sabbath, but these Pharisees and their teachers before them had so limited the right even of a physician to bring help on a Sabbath that he was permitted to do so only if the patient was in imminent danger of death. Compassion and mercy were totally ignored, except when it came to their lifestock. They had transformed the Sabbath commandment into a cruel and inflexible demand. The Lord in his answer in the former episode (2:27) had already attempted to set them straight. Deep in their hearts they knew that Christ was right, but in their hatred for him they refused to admit it.

That is the key to the next statement, one of but a few of its kind concerning our Lord: "He looked around at them in anger." (See also 10:14). If Jesus had not responded in righteous anger, he would have revealed a heart less than merciful, less than righteous. His anger was anything but sinful. It was combined with deep distress at their stubborn hearts, for they were not only violating the spiritual sense of the Sabbath but were also rejecting him as Savior. "He came to that which was his own, but his own did not receive him" (John 1:11).

The Lord did not touch the man's shriveled hand or speak a word of healing. He simply said, "Stretch out your hand," and the man was completely healed. Neither having spoken a word of healing nor having touched the man, Jesus technically could not be accused of violating the Pharisees' unscriptural Sabbath law. This outraged them more than ever, and they went out and plotted with the Herodians how to kill Jesus. Not only did they thereby violate the Sabbath commandment, for their hearts were not filled with thoughts of worship that day, but they also made themselves guilty of breaking the commandment: "You shall not murder" (Exodus 20:13).

Hatred makes strange bedfellows. In desperation they made common cause with the Herodians, Jews who supported Herod and the Roman government. Thus they were people whom the Pharisees would ordinarily have shunned. But in hating Christ and plotting his death they felt they needed the support of some able to wield secular power. They did the same later when Jesus was tried before Pontius Pilate. In our own world we run into similar alliances. That will never change.

Jesus' Later Galilean Ministry
Crowds Follow Jesus

[7]Jesus withdrew with his disciples to the lake, and a large crowd from Galilee followed. [8]When they heard all he was doing, many

people came to him from Judea, Jerusalem, Idumea, and the regions across the Jordan and around Tyre and Sidon. [9]Because of the crowd he told his disciples to have a small boat ready for him, to keep the people from crowding him. [10]For he had healed many, so that those with diseases were pushing forward to touch him. [11]Whenever the evil spirits saw him, they fell down before him and cried out, "You are the Son of God." [12]But he gave them strict orders not to tell who he was.

(Matthew 12:15,16; Luke 6:17-19)

With these words Mark summarizes Jesus' activity thus far in his ministry. Then follow his appointment of the twelve apostles and their instruction through parables and miracles in preparation for the day when the Lord would leave not only the synagogues and the cities, but this earth as well, and leave behind these men as his representatives. The disciples mentioned in verse 7 are more than just the Twelve.

In withdrawing to the lake region (Sea of Galilee, Mark 1:16; Lake of Gennesaret, Luke 5:1; Sea of Tiberias, John 21:1) and avoiding the synagogues Jesus showed his awareness of the plot being forged against him by the Pharisees. He also knew the time was not yet ripe for a head-on confrontation. There was still work to do, people to be brought into contact with the word and his disciples to train. It was not fear that caused Jesus to withdraw, but prudence and the determination to follow the Father's timetable.

His withdrawing from the urban setting did not stop the people from coming out to hear him and to see him. In fact, the crowds increased. How did they come to know of Jesus? Not only because he had preached the gospel and healed many sick throughout Galilee, but because those who had heard and seen him spoke of him. Whether the people then came out of curiosity or because they believed is beside the point. They came and heard and saw, and the Holy Spirit in his own good time brought the chosen to faith.

That's something for us to take to heart in our church life. The church is not a closed society, but one that always seeks to gain others. Therefore we must speak out in every possible way by making use of techniques and media modern science places at our disposal.

It was natural that many in the crowd following Jesus were from Galilee. That's where the Lord had concentrated his activity. But the news had spread. Many came from Judea, Jerusalem, Idumea, the regions across the Jordan River, and from Tyre and Sidon. Not all of these were necessarily Jews, nor did they necessarily speak the Aramaic language. That suggests that Christ, who grew up in Galilee where Greek was a second language, also was able and willing to speak to them in Greek, which most of them likely understood.

The church today speaks many languages. Missionaries of my church body proclaim the gospel in at least a half-dozen different tongues. Christ is the Savior of all, and all need the truth to be proclaimed to them. None know it of themselves.

This is evident when we take a look at the crowds which came to Christ. They kept coming not first of all because he proclaimed God's message, but because he could and did heal them. To such an extent they crowded the Lord and sought to touch him that he had to provide a safety valve. He asked the disciples to have a boat ready so that he could get away from the crowd.

Then there was the testimony of a certain group that he continued to reject, namely, the testimony of the evil spirits who caused those who were possessed by them to fall down before him and cry out, "You are the Son of God." For Christ at that moment to have accepted their testimony and made use of it would have played right into the hands of the Pharisees. Later in this chapter the teachers of the law from Jerusalem accused him of being "possessed by Beelzebub."

Though evil spirits were inappropriate witnesses, Mark includes their testimony so that we may know the evil spirits did indeed recognize Christ for what he is, the Son of God. For us, living in a different situation from that of Christ before his sacrificial suffering and death, their testimony —though they were not major witnesses — also assures us of the truth that Christ is the Son of God, particularly when we notice "they fell down before him and cried out." Their fear and terror remind us that Scripture states: "Even the demons believe that," namely, that there is one God, "and shudder" (James 2:19). But the people who were possessed by the demons were healed, and Satan could thus no longer use them as his instruments.

The Appointing of the Twelve Apostles

13Jesus went up on a mountainside and called to him those he wanted, and they came to him. 14He appointed twelve — designating them apostles — that they might be with him and that he might send them out to preach 15and to have authority to drive out demons. 16These are the twelve he appointed: Simon (to whom he gave the name Peter); 17James son of Zebedee and his brother John (to them he gave the name Boanerges, which means Sons of Thunder); 18Andrew, Philip, Bartholomew, Matthew, Thomas, James son of Alphaeus, Thaddaeus, Simon the Zealot 19and Judas Iscariot, who betrayed him.
(Matthew 10:2-4; Luke 6:12-16)

Matthew records the names of the Twelve in connection with their being sent out on their first preaching journey.

Luke, like Mark, gives us their names in connection with their being appointed as apostles by Christ.

During his ministry in Galilee and the surrounding areas, our Lord had many followers. They were not with him constantly, but would listen to his teaching every time he was in their vicinity or accompany him on some of his preaching journeys. Now the time had come for Jesus to organize his followers so that after he had completed his task here on earth and returned to the glory of heaven his church would have reliable leadership.

Luke relates in the appointment of the Twelve that Jesus spent the whole previous night in prayer. Mark leaves no doubt as to what the specific duties of the Twelve would be both in the immediate present and in the future. They are to preach the gospel and drive out demons, the latter because salvation involved the overcoming of Satan and his angels.

The appointment of the Twelve was not something the Lord did in secret, but in the presence of a large group of followers and disciples whom the Lord had summoned to meet with him in the Galilean hills. He wanted his apostles to have the full support and confidence of their fellow believers.

As we look at the Twelve, we must admit they were a rather diverse group. None of them were priests or teachers of the law. None were people in high standing in Israel. For the most part they were common, ordinary, working people.

Simon Peter always heads the list. He was a man of action and quick decision, always ready to speak for the disciples as a group. Christ gave him the name Peter, which means rock, not because he always was a rock, but because he indeed was a rock when he let his faith in Jesus speak and act. His lowest hour was when he denied Christ, and probably his highest hour when he preached that powerful sermon on Pentecost and three thousand turned to the Lord. Though Scripture never places him in Rome for twenty-five years as bishop or pope, he perhaps died a martyr's death in Rome. Peter wrote two epistles which are included in the New Testament.

James and John, the sons of Zebedee, were called "Boanerges" by Christ, meaning Sons of Thunder. A burning zeal for their Lord characterized them. At times they were too ambitious for their own good (10:35-41). James was the first of the apostles to lay down his life for his faith in Jesus. He was arrested by Herod Agrippa in the year A.D. 42 and beheaded. John was the writer of the Gospel that bears his name, three letters in the New Testament and the Book of Revelation. He outlived all the other apostles.

Andrew shared with John the honor of being the first followers of Jesus. According to John 1:40-42 it was he who brought his brother Simon Peter to Jesus. Andrew and John had been disciples of John the Baptist.

Philip was from Bethsaida, the hometown of Andrew and Peter before they moved to Capernaum, possibly when Peter was married. On the day after Simon Peter was brought to Jesus by Andrew, Jesus himself asked Philip to follow him. And Philip immediately brought Nathanael to Jesus.

Nathanael, or Bartholomew, was the first to voice the conviction: "Rabbi, you are the Son of God; you are the King of Israel" (John 1:49). The Evangelist John calls him by his given name, Nathanael, whereas the other Gospel writers speak of him as Bartholomew, a patronymic meaning "son of Talmai or Ptolemy." The Gospels do not tell us a great deal about either Philip or Bartholomew, but tradition has it that Philip did mission work in Asia Minor, and Bartholomew took the gospel as far as India.

Matthew is Levi, about whom Mark wrote in chapter 2, a tax collector in Herod's service and thus a man whom the religious aristocracy of the Jews had absolutely no use for. But Jesus appointed him an apostle, and he later wrote the first Gospel.

Thomas, Didymus in Greek and named so three times in John's Gospel, was a man who would not accept anything as fact until it was demonstrated to him, somewhat like many in this modern era. It took visible, tangible proof to convince Thomas of the resurrection of Christ. But when it was offered by the Lord himself, Thomas replied, "My Lord and my God!" Thus, if there is any one man who guarantees the account of our Lord's redemptive acts is factual, he is Thomas. Modern man, insistent on tangible proof, needs him among the apostles. Jesus provided him. Today we would therefore say, A good choice!

All we know about the next apostle, James, is that he was the son of Alphaeus. Scripture mentions him only in the lists of the apostles Jesus chose. Thus we know that he was present at and after the ascension of our Lord. But just because we know no more about him does not mean that he was a nonentity or a failure. As so many unsung heroes of the Christian church, he also did the work the Lord called him to perform.

Thaddaeus is another apostle about whom we know next to nothing. Mark undoubtedly used the name Thaddaeus to distinguish him from Judas Iscariot. Matthew also calls him Thaddaeus, though some Greek texts of Matthew call him Lebbaeus. See Matthew 10:3 (KJV). Luke calls him Judas son of James.

A startling choice on the part of Jesus was Simon the Zealot. He was called the Zealot undoubtedly because he had been a member of a patriotic Jewish rebel party by that name. Others translate the term as the Cananaean or the Patriot, but the meaning is the same. Jesus could use a man of ardor in spreading the gospel once his loyalty had been switched from a political messiah to the heavenly Messiah.

The saddest name is the last, Judas Iscariot, who betrayed him. His home town was Kerioth, making him the only apostle who came from Judea. At the beginning undoubtedly a faithful follower of Jesus, he became disillusioned, filled his pockets from the common purse, betrayed the Lord and finally committed suicide. Jesus frequently but unsuccessfully tried to turn him from the fatal path he had chosen, but he persisted and thus fulfilled the tragic role Ahitophel had played in the life of King David (see Psalm 41:9; John 13:18). We are not told when Judas fell from faith, but this much we can be certain of, namely, that Jesus did not choose him in order to have him commit this heinous crime. We know that Jesus as God the Son knows all things in advance, and yet he chose this man not to have him betray him, but to preach and teach the gospel. He was the Lord's greatest disappointment. "Judas, are you betraying the Son of Man with a kiss?" We see tears running down our Savior's face. Admittedly this is a mystery, but at the same time a warning.

The Twelve were a mixed group — two pairs of brothers, four fishermen, all but one Galileans, one a tax collector and another a past member of a rebel political party. All had differing spiritual gifts. Some became prominent in the life of the New Testament church; others remained totally in the background. All but one experienced the comfort and strength of the passion, resurrection and ascension of Christ, and all but one were ready to go wherever the Lord would send them. But before this could take place, the Lord had to train them and then complete his own task of saving you and me and them and of paying for the sins of the world. None of this is fiction; all is real. In reading Mark's Gospel we are thrilled to walk in their footsteps.

Jesus Defends Himself Against the Accusation of Possession by Beelzebub

20Then Jesus entered a house, and again a crowd gathered, so that he and his disciples were not even able to eat. 21When his family heard about this, they went to take charge of him, for they said, "He is out of his mind."

22And the teachers of the law who came down from Jerusalem said, "He is possessed by Beelzebub! By the prince of demons he is driving out demons."

23So Jesus called them and spoke to them in parables: "How can Satan drive out Satan? 24If a kingdom is divided against itself, that kingdom cannot stand. 25If a house is divided against itself, that house cannot stand. 26And if Satan opposes himself and is divided, he cannot stand; his end has come. 27In fact, no one can enter a strong man's house and carry off his possessions unless he first ties up the strong man. Then he can rob his house. 28I tell you the truth, all the sins and blasphemies of men will be forgiven them. 29But whoever blasphemes against the Holy Spirit will never be forgiven; he is guilty of an eternal sin."

30He said this because they were saying, "He has an evil spirit."
(Matthew 12:24-32; Luke 11:15-23)

In this section the opposition to Christ comes to a head on the part of both his family and the teachers of the law. His answer includes some of the most explicit warnings from the mouth of the Son of Man while here on earth. We do well to take them to heart.

Jesus had returned to his home in Capernaum, evidently after a longer preaching journey. He and his disciples needed rest and food. But no sooner was his presence known than crowds gathered, so that he and his disciples could not even find time to eat. That's when his family said, "Enough!" and gathered to talk some sense into him or to restrain him forcibly. "It's insane and unhealthy how he's spending him-

55

self. He doesn't seem to be concerned about the welfare of his disciples, to say nothing about himself. We've got to do something." Perhaps they meant well, but their actions and attitude reveal they did not believe in him as the promised Savior. Nor did they understand the necessity of his using every possible opportunity of sharing his message, particularly in view of the opposition he was meeting on the part of the religious leaders. It is possible that Mary the mother of Jesus summoned the brothers and family members together, for she appears with them in verse 31.

If the family members had serious misgivings, the teachers of the law went all out in seeking to undermine Christ's influence. The opportunity was given them, according to Matthew 12:22, when a demon-possessed man who was blind and mute was brought to Christ and he healed him. Lest the people now believe in Christ, the teachers of the law spoke up and said, "He is possessed by Beelzebub! By the prince of demons he is driving out demons." Beelzebub, meaning "lord of flies" and mocking the name of a Philistine idol, was a popular name for Satan. The religious teachers should have recognized by this time what was really taking place, namely, Jesus was fulfilling the prophecies of the Old Testament. But they closed their eyes to that and instead slandered and blasphemed Christ publicly. Their accusations demanded a public, no-nonsense answer from Jesus.

Christ's answer was metaphorical, in the form of parables. The first part of Christ's answer was an appeal to their logic, their common sense. "How can Satan drive out Satan?" That's the last thing Satan would want to do.

Christ here assures his hearers and Mark's readers down to this day that Satan actually exists, contrary to so many theologians today who deny both Satan and hell. Christ also knows of no second chance after death, of no purgatory.

Christ then proceeded with his logical exposure of their argument. A kingdom divided, caught up in a civil war, won't stand — nor a family divided, or a dynasty divided. Satan would be crazy to oppose himself.

When Christ next stated that to rob a strong man's house a robber must first tie up the strong man, it's clear he was referring to his own actions. That's exactly what Christ did when he robbed Satan of many who had been possessed by Satan's minions. For the strongest evidence we need only think back to Jesus' first encounter with Satan after his baptism (1:12,13). There Satan had suffered a total defeat, in a sense he had been tied up.

Jesus' answer was simple logic and his opponents should have recognized its truth, but they had set their hearts against Jesus and, in this case, against the work of the Spirit of God. That's why Jesus now uttered a sharp warning: "You have blasphemed me. That can indeed be forgiven. But if you blaspheme the Holy Spirit, that can never be forgiven." Thus he warned them that they had come very close to the sin against the Holy Spirit. In the case of many others, for example, the members of his own family, it had simply been honest doubt, misunderstanding, and being puzzled, but in their case it was coming dangerously close to hardening their hearts to the testimony of the Holy Spirit. The difference becomes evident when we compare Peter's denial of Christ and Caiaphas's verdict pronounced on Christ.

When people deliberately identify Christ with Satan and speak of his work as satanic, the Holy Spirit can no longer do his work in their hearts, the work of bringing them to faith in Jesus Christ as their Savior. When the Pharisees speak of the Spirit in Christ as satanic, they are indeed close to having committed the sin that cannot be forgiven. But those who in their hearts are troubled whether they are guilty of this sin can be sure that they have not committed it. Their concern shows the Spirit is still carrying on his work in their hearts. Nor can we pass judgment on others; only God knows. We, on our part, must continue to warn against it, even as Jesus did.

The English translation of verse 28 does not quite bring out the seriousness of Jesus' words. The Greek words translated, "I tell you the truth," are much more emphatic. They read: "Amen (the truth), I tell you." Jesus in the Gospels repeatedly uses this expression. In Mark it occurs at least twelve times.

Jesus' Mother and Brothers

31 Then Jesus' mother and brothers arrived. Standing outside, they sent someone in to call him. 32 A crowd was sitting around him, and they told him, "Your mother and brothers are outside looking for you."

33 "Who are my mother and my brothers?" he asked.

34 Then he looked at those seated in a circle around him and said, "Here are my mother and my brothers! 35 Whoever does God's will is my brother and sister and mother."

(Matthew 12:46-50; Luke 8:19-21)

From verse 21 we know their purpose. His family felt Jesus was not acting rationally in devoting himself so fully to his work. Of his brothers Acts 1:14 records they later came to faith in him. There is no reason to include Mary among those who at this time did not believe in him. As a fully human mother she was concerned about the stress and strain Jesus was evidently subject to. However when she and Jesus' brothers took this action, they were asserting a responsibility they did not have, though their intentions were good. It was interference on their part in his messianic work.

The brothers of Jesus were the children of Mary and Joseph and born after Jesus' own virgin birth. To insist that Mary and Joseph were celibate after the birth of Jesus is to insist on something not taught by Scripture.

Mary and his brothers sent a messenger to Jesus through the crowd. This gave him an opportunity to express a truth they and all of us need to take to heart — how we too become Jesus' brothers and sisters. Jesus' question, "Who are my mother and my brothers?" was designed to gain the attention of those around him, also of his mother and brothers. He answered his own question by pointing to those seated around him — his disciples, undoubtedly more than the Twelve. "Here are my mother and brothers," he said. In saying so he was not rejecting his own flesh and blood, but pointing out that in the kingdom of God, the church, there is something much more important than human relationship. He defined his family thus: "Whoever does God's will is my brother and sister and mother."

What is this will of God? Is it the law as such, the Ten Commandments, and possibly the ramifications added by the teachers of the law? Then none of us would qualify, also none of Jesus' own disciples. The will of God is that will as expressed in Jesus Christ and his redemptive act. It is the supreme truth expressed in that most loved of all Bible passages, John 3:16: "For God so loved the world that he gave his one and only Son, that whoever believes in him shall not perish but have eternal life." Then John continues: "For God did not send his Son into the world to condemn the world, but to save the world through him." Doing the will of God is believing and trusting in what he has done for us through Christ Jesus. That will also bring with it a love for all the other commands of our God.

Your being a child of God — a brother, sister or mother of Jesus Christ — has no restrictions as to race, color, nationality, sex, age or handicap. That family relationship is offered to all. Here is the invitation, and you are invited.

The Parable of the Sower

4 Again Jesus began to teach by the lake. The crowd that gathered around him was so large that he got into a boat and sat in it out on the lake, while all the people were along the shore at the water's edge. ²He taught them many things by parables, and in his teaching said: ³"Listen! A farmer went out to sow his seed. ⁴As he was scattering the seed, some fell along the path, and the birds came and ate it up. ⁵Some fell on rocky places, where it did not have much soil. It sprang up quickly, because the soil was shallow. ⁶But when the sun came up, the plants were scorched, and they withered because they had no root. ⁷Other seed fell among thorns, which grew up and choked the plants, so that they did not bear grain. ⁸Still other seed fell on good soil. It came up, grew and produced a crop, multiplying thirty, sixty or even a hundred times."

⁹Then Jesus said, "He who has ears to hear, let him hear."

¹⁰When he was alone, the Twelve and the others around him asked him about the parables. ¹¹He told them, "The secret of the kingdom of God has been given to you. But to those on the outside everything is said in parables ¹²so that,

" 'they may be ever seeing but not perceiving,
and ever hearing but never understanding;
otherwise they might turn and be forgiven!' "

¹³Then Jesus said to them, "Don't you understand this parable? How then will you understand any parable? ¹⁴The farmer sows the word. ¹⁵Some people are like seed along the path, where the word is sown. As soon as they hear it, Satan comes and takes away the word that was sown in them. ¹⁶Others, like seed sown on rocky places, hear the word and at once receive it with joy. ¹⁷But since they have no root, they last only a short time. When trouble or persecution comes because of the word, they quickly fall away. ¹⁸Still others, like seed sown among thorns, hear the word; ¹⁹but

the worries of this life, the deceitfulness of wealth and the desires for other things come in and choke the word, making it unfruitful. [20]Others, like seed sown on good soil, hear the word, accept it, and produce a crop — thirty, sixty or even a hundred times what was sown."

(Matthew 13:1-23; Luke 8:4-15)

Although Mark has presented Jesus as teacher from the very beginning of his Gospel, he has not recorded many of the discussions in detail, but put more emphasis on the miracles Jesus performed and on the opposition he encountered. As the fury of the opposition increased, Jesus took more and more to speaking in parables. Mark devotes almost this entire chapter to parables Jesus told. By speaking in parables the Lord left his opponents without an immediate answer. But the parables gave them occasion to ponder his answer and eventually to come up with an appropriate answer for themselves. At least that is what Jesus had in mind.

A parable as used by Jesus was an earthly story giving expression to a spiritual truth. Parables were nothing new; Nathan used one in speaking to David in 2 Samuel 12:1-4. As used by Jesus, most of them were directly connected with his person and his redemptive work. Though the parables were not always transparent in expressing the truth, it was not our Lord's purpose to withhold the truth, but to compel the hearers to dig for it. Jesus, as we see here and in previous chapters, was a master in the use of parables and seems to have spoken them often on the spur of the moment.

On this occasion Jesus again was in Galilee at the lake. The crowd was so large that as before (3:9) Jesus felt compelled to escape in a boat. He sat in the boat out on the lake and instructed the people who were along the shore. Clearly Jesus must have had a voice that carried well.

Jesus told his audience a number of parables on this day. The first of these was the Parable of the Sower. In connection with it Mark has recorded what Jesus later that day, after the crowd had gone, told his disciples concerning his use of parables and their purpose.

The illustrations used by Jesus were familiar to his audience. They had all seen farmers sow their seed, had perhaps done so themselves. Some seed, as the farmers scattered it by hand, was bound to fall on paths, on rocky places and among thorns, besides on the good soil prepared to receive it. Jesus began his parable with the word "Listen!" and ended it by saying, "He who has ears to hear, let him hear." It's clear he was not having an instruction class for farmers. His purpose was no different than ever before, and we can't help but imagine the subsequent discussion: "Just what spiritual truth does he want us to learn? What's the seed? What are the birds, the rocky place, the thorns? What makes the soil good?" Perhaps quite a few came up with some very acceptable answers.

However the Twelve and other disciples later asked Jesus to explain this parable and especially his reason for speaking in parables. He told them first of all he was not withholding any truth from them: "The secret of the kingdom of God has been given to you." The mystery of the kingdom is the good news that God in his dealing with men has now sent the One who will be the Savior and Redeemer, and that that One is Christ. During the time of the Old Testament this coming One had been promised; now it could be revealed that he had indeed come and begun his work. Even so, the mystery was as yet not an open book. Only after the resurrection and ascension would the disciples understand more fully.

However some who heard Christ would never come to an understanding. As evidence he quoted (verse 12) the words of Isaiah 6:9,10. In Isaiah's ministry the time had come when

God through the preaching of Isaiah hardened the hearts of many in Israel as a just and righteous punishment. Jesus recognized that a similar time had also come in his own ministry. But nowhere did Jesus say these words of Isaiah applied to everyone of his hearers.

Nor does Jesus here say we in our ministry today can apply these words to our hearers. Only God can make a judgment like that. We cannot look into the hearts of people. To the Twelve when he sends them out to preach Jesus says, "And if any place will not welcome you or listen to you, shake the dust off your feet when you leave, as a testimony against them" (6:11). But the door for repentance is still ajar. And that's why the Christians' present assignment reads: "Preach the good news to all creation" (16:15).

When Jesus turns to explaining the parable to his disciples, it is evident he is disappointed they have not understood it. The explanation is very simple. It alerts us to the foes which attack the preaching of the word and its hearing — Satan, trouble, persecution, the worries of life, the deceitfulness of wealth and the desires (lust) for other things. All these can come between the hearer and the message and rob the hearer of faith. All preachers have seen exact counterparts of what Christ here told his disciples. But, Christ adds, there is always success too. The word never returns void. The good soil produces thirty, sixty or even a hundred times what is sown.

The one point Jesus does not explain here is how we become good soil. Certainly, not of ourselves. By nature we are lost in trespasses and sins. It is God's grace that opens our hearts to hear and believe the word and enables us to bring forth the fruits of faith. The parable calls on us who hear the word to be on guard against everything that would seek to rob us of becoming a fruitful field. To us also

apply the words Jesus spoke to the multitude: "Listen! ...
He who has ears to hear, let him hear." Our ears too are
God's gifts.

This parable also comforts the faithful pastors as it later
did the apostles and disciples. All they are called upon to do
is to sow the seed. They are not responsible for the harvest.
The Spirit will produce that through the seed, and it will not
all be the same. Some will be thirty, some sixty, some a
hundred times. Despite all opposition there will be a harvest.

A Lamp on a Stand

**21He said to them, "Do you bring in a lamp to put it under a
bowl or a bed? Instead, don't you put it on its stand? 22For
whatever is hidden is meant to be disclosed, and whatever is
concealed is meant to be brought out into the open. 23If anyone
has ears to hear, let him hear."**

**24"Consider carefully what you hear," he continued. "With the
measure you use, it will be measured to you — and even more.
25Whoever has will be given more; whoever does not have, even
what he has will be taken from him."**

(Matthew 5:15; Luke 8:16-18; 11:33)

After interrupting his account to tell how Jesus explained
the parable to the disciples and why Jesus spoke in parables,
Mark records other parables our Lord spoke that day. They
are all familiar because we find similar statements spoken by
our Lord recorded in the other Gospels. In other words,
Jesus frequently made use of similar illustrations, but did
not always make the same application.

The seed in the first parable is the word proclaimed by
Jesus and later to be proclaimed by his disciples down to our
day. This word produces a crop or, as this parable puts it,
lights a lamp. What is to be done with a lamp when it is lit? It

certainly is not to be placed under a bowl or under a bed, but is to be put on a stand so that it may give light. Men often seek to cover up their deeds, hoping they will never be revealed. They will not succeed in doing so, since on judgment day all things will be revealed. But Jesus wants his word, the account of his deeds, proclaimed. That light began to shine in its full glory on Pentecost. The Book of Acts tells the story, as does the history of the church.

In the next words our Lord alerts believers not to take this matter of being a light and sharing the good news haphazardly, for the same measure we use in sharing it with others will be used toward us. Sharing the gospel leads into searching the Bible. The more we search it, the deeper our insight into the blessings of God's gospel. Neglecting worship and the Word leads only to a diminished supply. And finally, unless such repent and recharge their batteries, their light will go out. Ernest Hemingway, brought up by Christian parents, later in life in a letter to one of his family wrote, "Oh, yes, I still believe in Christ, but don't tell anyone." We know how he lived and died — a suicide.

The Parable of the Growing Seed

²⁶He also said, "This is what the kingdom of God is like. A man scatters seed on the ground. ²⁷Night and day, whether he sleeps or gets up, the seed sprouts and grows, though he does not know how. ²⁸All by itself the soil produces grain — first the stalk, then the head, then the full kernel in the head. ²⁹As soon as the grain is ripe, he puts the sickle to it, because the harvest has come."

This parable is found only in Mark.

Whenever Christ speaks about the kingdom of God, his ruling activity, his words always have something to do with the seed, the gospel that brings men to faith in Christ Jesus. Here Jesus speaks of the power and reliability of the gospel message. All that need be done, in fact, all that can be done, is to sow the seed, to proclaim the word. A farmer who plants the seed does not understand how it grows. The power is in the seed. So it is with the gospel. It is sown; it sprouts; it matures; it is harvested. Christ's words echo Isaiah 55:11: "So is my word that goes out from my mouth: It will not return to me empty, but will accomplish what I desire and achieve the purpose for which I sent it."

The harvest includes the final harvest at the end of the world, when all mankind will see the marvelous fruit the Lord produced through his word in this world of sin. But the harvest is also reaped here and now in the life of every child of God in whose heart the word has taken root and grown, and whose faith God uses time and time again to bring that same word to others. The harvest isn't the believer's doing, but God's. Thus this parable was of special comfort to the apostles as they carried out Jesus' assignment. Paul later put it this way in 1 Corinthians 3:6,7: "I planted the seed, Apollos watered it, but God made it grow. So neither he who plants nor he who waters is anything, but only God, who makes things grow." Though at times we may not see the results, there will be a harvest because the seed has God's power within it.

One thing must still be noted. When the NIV translates "all by itself" (v 28) and the KJV "the earth ... of herself," it might seem as though the earth (the human heart) receives some credit. Not at all, for the Greek really means "spontaneously," "automatically," or "as a matter of course." The person's heart is only the locale where it takes place. God's power inherent in the word is the cause. If it were not so, you and I would be without hope, for by nature we are corrupt and sinful, and we reject the grace of God. It is God alone who overcomes this opposition on our part and brings us to faith. We preach and teach the word; God's word does the rest.

The Parable of the Mustard Seed

³⁰Again he said, "What shall we say the kingdom of God is like, or what parable shall we use to describe it? ³¹It is like a mustard seed, which is the smallest seed you plant in the ground. ³²Yet when planted, it grows and becomes the largest of all garden plants, with such big branches that the birds of the air can perch in its shade."

(Matthew 13:31,32; Luke 13:18,19)

Jesus opened this presentation with two questions. He wanted his hearers, and especially his disciples, to give this matter diligent thought. Thus he gained their attention.

Again the activity spoken of here was the preaching of the gospel. Jesus acknowledged that looked at from the worldly point of view this was no big deal. It was a kingdom without a realm, without armies, certainly without an imposing king. When Christ proclaimed the word, the leading men of his nation — the priests, the Pharisees, the teachers of the law, the rich Sadducees — did not follow him. They ridiculed him, and undoubtedly that often troubled his hearers. Even the apostles had many misconceptions (see Acts 1:6). They needed to take another look at this and similar parables.

The kingdom of God is not one of outward form and shape. Its New Testament beginnings were so small as to be almost invisible. But Christ kept telling his disciples, "Don't be disturbed; the eternal fruits will be large indeed." That's the parallel parable of the mustard seed, the smallest of all seeds usually planted, which becomes the largest of all garden plants, sometimes reaching a height of eight to ten feet, large enough for birds to perch in its shade. We cannot judge the final size of the kingdom by the initial size of the seed. The gospel has extraordinary power and vitality.

A Summary Statement

³³With many similar parables Jesus spoke the word to them, as much as they could understand. ³⁴He did not say anything to them without using a parable. But when he was alone with his own disciples, he explained everything.

Mark does not say that Jesus spoke only in parables, but that whenever he spoke to the people he made use of parables. But let's not forget that his hearers did have the Old Testament. Christ used parables because they often matched the hearers' degree of understanding, also because the gospel had not been consummated. Until then Jesus could not speak more clearly than he did.

To the apostles and the disciples who had confessed him he explained the parables more thoroughly. But when Jesus began to foretell his suffering and death, even the apostles did not understand and tried to dissuade him right up to the last moment in the Garden of Gethsemane. How different was their spirit when all had been completed and when Christ had sent his Spirit upon them! And their preaching was also different — no parables, but one gospel truth after another. That's also when these parables became real words of wisdom for them and many others. For the present, however, for Christ to have taught otherwise than in parables might have resulted in interference with God's plan of salvation (John 6:14,15). It's the same kind of situation as when he forbade evil spirits (1:34) and those possessed by them (1:25) to testify that he was the Son of God.

Jesus Calms the Storm

³⁵That day when evening came, he said to his disciples, "Let us go over to the other side." ³⁶Leaving the crowd behind, they took him along, just as he was, in the boat. There were also other boats with him. ³⁷A furious squall came up, and the waves broke over

Stilling the Storm

the boat, so that it was nearly swamped. ³⁸Jesus was in the stern, sleeping on a cushion. The disciples woke him and said to him, "Teacher, don't you care if we drown?"

³⁹He got up, rebuked the wind and said to the waves, "Quiet! Be still!" Then the wind died down and it was completely calm.

⁴⁰He said to his disciples, "Why are you so afraid? Do you still have no faith?"

⁴¹They were terrified and asked each other, "Who is this? Even the wind and the waves obey him!"

(Matthew 8:18,23-27; Luke 8:22-25)

It had been a strenuous day. When evening came, the Lord was ready to be alone with his disciples and away from the crowd. He was tired, but he also knew there was someone desperately in need of his help on the other side of the lake. In the meantime there was also a lesson to be taught to his disciples.

The Sea of Galilee, surrounded by high hills as it is, is subject to sudden storms. While Jesus was asleep in the stern of the boat with his head on a pillow — see his true humanity! — a sudden squall struck. So furious were the waves that they threatened to swamp the boat. The storm was extraordinary, as shown by the reaction of the disciples. Experienced fishermen though they were, they could not control the boat and feared for their lives. In their great fear they woke Christ, and their words to him were words both of faith and of rebuke. They believed he could help them, but why had he not taken a hand already? It seemed to them as though he did not care. Their faith was not thinking straight. They were not applying to their situation all they had witnessed him do previously.

Christ gave them an answer that definitely showed them he was not only a man in touch with God, but himself possessed the power of God. At creation God spoke the word, and it was so. Here Jesus Christ spoke, "Quiet! Be still!" and the wind and the waves obeyed. In fact, the waves died down immediately, something that normally did not happen. The calm was complete.

Christ's next words forced the disciples to face their own spiritual weakness: "Why are you so afraid? Do you still have no faith?" They should have known by this time that by having Christ on board with them awake or asleep they were safe. They had called him teacher, but had not taken his teachings to heart. They learned from this experience, and we should too. The world we live in is still under the control of our Savior, its Creator.

For the moment awe and wonder fill the hearts of the disciples. "Who is this?" It's the one whom wind and waves must obey. He is more than a man; he is the very Son of God. Their faith has been permitted to grow.

As we read this account, we are particularly struck by all the details Mark gives, as compared with the other Gospels. Such details could only be supplied by an eyewitness, Mark's mentor, the Apostle Peter.

What happened to the other boats? Perhaps they turned back as Jesus and his apostles pulled out. At any rate the Lord, who saved the disciples, would also have saved them, had they been in danger. That the Lord Jesus came to the rescue of his disciples and did not permit those in the other boats to perish, however, must not be misused by us. To expect the Lord to come through for us when we knowingly take unnecessary and uncalled for risks is not applying faith in our Lord's actions on the Sea of Galilee properly. In that case it was the Lord himself who told his disciples, "Let us go over to the other side." It had not been their own idea, nor did they know in advance that a storm was brewing and thus deliberately took a chance.

The Healing of a Demon-possessed Man

5 They went across the lake to the region of the Gerasenes. ²When Jesus got out of the boat, a man with an evil spirit came from the tombs to meet him. ³This man lived in the tombs, and no one could bind him any more, not even with a chain. ⁴For he had often been chained hand and foot, but he tore the chains apart and broke the irons on his feet. No one was strong enough to subdue him. ⁵Night and day among the tombs and in the hills he would cry out and cut himself with stones.

⁶When he saw Jesus from a distance, he ran and fell on his knees in front of him. ⁷He shouted at the top of his voice, "What do you want with me, Jesus, Son of the Most High God? Swear to God that you won't torture me!" ⁸For Jesus had said to him, "Come out of this man, you evil spirit!"

⁹Then Jesus asked him, "What is your name?"

"My name is Legion," he replied, "for we are many." ¹⁰And he begged Jesus again and again not to send them out of the area.

¹¹A large herd of pigs was feeding on the nearby hillside. ¹²The demons begged Jesus, "Send us among the pigs; allow us to go into them." ¹³He gave them permission, and the evil spirits came out and went into the pigs. The herd, about two thousand in number, rushed down the steep bank into the lake and were drowned.

¹⁴Those tending the pigs ran off and reported this in the town and countryside, and the people went out to see what had happened. ¹⁵When they came to Jesus, they saw the man who had been possessed by the legion of demons, sitting there, dressed and in his right mind; and they were afraid. ¹⁶Those who had seen it told the people what had happened to the demon-possessed man — and told about the pigs as well. ¹⁷Then the people began to plead with Jesus to leave their region.

¹⁸As Jesus was getting into the boat, the man who had been demon-possessed begged to go with him. ¹⁹Jesus did not let him, but said, "Go home to your family and tell them how much the Lord has done for you, and how he has had mercy on you." ²⁰So

the man went away and began to tell in the Decapolis how much Jesus had done for him. And all the people were amazed.
(Matthew 8;28-34; Luke 8:26-39)

Can he who stilled the storm on the lake also still the storms in people's hearts? Can he meet our spiritual needs as well as our physical needs? Come across the lake and see.

The territory on the eastern side of the lake was predominantly mixed — Gentiles and Jews. Mark and Luke called it the region of the Gerasenes, and Matthew the region of the Gadarenes. Gadara was one of the main cities in the territory called Decapolis ("ten cities"). Another was Gerasa. So all three evangelists were speaking about the same territory. Each of them also added details all his own. Matthew wrote that there were two demon-possessed men. Mark and Luke, who zero in on the one who spoke, did not say that there was only one. At the place where the boat pulled to land there was a cliff, and also many tombs.

Demon possession is not a mental aberration, but a condition in which a person is possessed by an evil mind and will not his own. How dreadful demon possession is becomes clear from Mark's description. There's a saying, "No rest for the wicked!" Satan gives this man no rest whatsoever day and night. The physical pain and torture — Mark tells us he cut himself with stones — is as great as the spiritual.

But one more powerful than Satan had come into the territory, and the demons acknowledged it. As soon as the man saw Jesus, he came and fell on his knees before him. This was not an act of worship, but simply an act whereby he acknowledged Jesus as the greater, as superior. He knew who Jesus was, for he screamed, "Jesus, Son of the Most High God." The demon knew that Jesus' mission was to overcome Satan and his cohorts. He knew what his own fate was, for he said, "Swear to God that you won't torture me."

And he begged Christ not to send him out of the area, that is, as both Matthew and Luke indicate, not to send him back to hell.

Questioned by Jesus — remember the disciples were with Jesus, and for them it was a learning experience — he said his name was Legion. A Roman army legion consisted of 6,000 soldiers. So Jesus was not dealing with just one demon but many. When they begged permission to enter a herd of about 2,000 pigs that were feeding on a nearby hillside, Jesus gave them permission. Possessed by the demons, the pigs rushed down a steep bank into the lake and drowned. Demons are alway destructive.

The owners of the pigs — Gentiles and apostate Jews —did not accuse Jesus of destroying their property. The Jews recognized by owning and raising these pigs they were violating the Old Testament ceremonial regulations and thus demonstrating they were no longer true believers. The Gentiles also suffered considerable financial loss and feared such a display of power. The owners had not heard the words of the demon-possessed man concerning Christ, but when they saw the man sitting there dressed and in his right mind and heard from eyewitnesses what all had happened, they were afraid. They should have been happy for the man who was healed and should have praised God with him, but: "Then the people began to plead with Jesus to leave their region." There are also any number of people today who do not welcome Jesus into their lives because he cramps their life-style.

So Jesus left; he did not force himself on anyone. The man who was healed begged to go with Jesus, but this was not possible because Jesus had an important task for him. Jesus left this man behind as his witness. The man shared with his family and all in the Decapolis the good news of what the Lord had done for him. Those who heard him were amazed, and many of them were Gentiles. The man carried out his task very well, for the next time Jesus came into this territory he was not asked to leave, but was welcomed (see Matthew 15:29-31 and Mark 7:31-36). So the first stop in Decapolis was an important one for our Lord; he won a witness for himself in predominantly Gentile territory.

All of us have relatives, friends, acquaintances and neighbors who are in just as dire straits as these people in the Decapolis. They face the same fate unless they are brought to Christ. They need our intercession and our witness. We can be for them what the former demon-possessed man was for the people of the Decapolis. Let them know how much Christ the Lord has done for us and is willing to do for them.

A Dead Girl and a Sick Woman

21 When Jesus had again crossed over by boat to the other side of the lake, a large crowd gathered around him while he was by the lake. 22 Then one of the synagogue rulers, named Jairus, came there. Seeing Jesus, he fell at his feet 23 and pleaded earnestly with him, "My little daughter is dying. Please come and put your hands on her so that she will be healed and live." 24 So Jesus went with him.

A large crowd followed and pressed around him. 25 And a woman was there who had been subject to bleeding for twelve years. 26 She had suffered a great deal under the care of many doctors and had spent all she had, yet instead of getting better she grew worse. 27 When she heard about Jesus, she came up behind him in the crowd and touched his cloak, 28 because she thought, "If I just touch his clothes, I will be healed." 29 Immediately her bleeding stopped and she felt in her body that she was freed from her suffering.

30 At once Jesus realized that power had gone out from him. He turned around in the crowd and asked, "Who touched my clothes?"

³¹"You see the people crowding against you," his disciples answered, "and yet you can ask, 'Who touched me?' "

³²But Jesus kept looking around to see who had done it. ³³Then the woman, knowing what had happened to her, came and fell at his feet and, trembling with fear, told him the whole truth. ³⁴He said to her, "Daughter, your faith has healed you. Go in peace and be freed from your suffering."

³⁵While Jesus was still speaking, some men came from the house of Jairus, the synagogue ruler. "Your daughter is dead," they said. "Why bother the teacher any more?"

³⁶Ignoring what they said, Jesus told the synagogue ruler, "Don't be afraid; just believe."

³⁷He did not let anyone follow him except Peter, James and John the brother of James. ³⁸When they came to the home of the synagogue ruler, Jesus saw a commotion, with people crying and wailing loudly. ³⁹He went in and said to them, "Why all this commotion and wailing? The child is not dead but asleep." ⁴⁰But they laughed at him.

After he put them all out, he took the child's father and mother and the disciples who were with him, and went in where the child was. ⁴¹He took her by the hand and said to her, "*Talitha koum!*" (which means, "Little girl, I say to you, get up!"). ⁴²Immediately the girl stood up and walked around (she was twelve years old). At this they were completely astonished. ⁴³He gave strict orders not to let anyone know about this, and told them to give her something to eat.

(Matthew 9:18-26; Luke 8:41-56)

Jairus's Plea in Behalf of His Daughter

Papias the church father, a disciple of the Apostle John, wrote that John told him that Mark "wrote accurately, though not in order, all that he remembered" hearing Peter say about Jesus. Mark often put together accounts that emphasize the same thing, here a number of accounts that demonstrate Jesus' miraculous power. Matthew, on the other hand, recorded that Jesus, after healing the two demon-possessed men, came back over the lake and returned to Capernaum. There he healed a paralytic, called Matthew (Levi) as his disciple, had dinner with tax collectors and "sinners" in Matthew's home, returned to the lake and there had a discussion with John the Baptist's disciples concerning fasting. It was then that Jairus came to him. Mark had already mentioned these events in chapter 2. It is clear that he had a different purpose, and in this case did not follow the chronological order.

We should be aware of this so that in comparing the Gospels we do not look for contradictions where there are none. Rather, let's search for the purpose these writers had when they recorded specific events. It is quite different when it comes to the record of the Holy Week. There the order in all the Gospels is chronological, although again none of them record all the details, but just those the Holy Spirit inspired them to include for the purpose for which they were writing.

Matthew compresses the account and has Jairus say, "My daughter is dead." Mark includes what actually took place. Jairus says, "My little daughter is dying." Somewhat later men come from his home to tell Jairus, "Your daughter is dead." Matthew simply calls attention to Jesus' miraculous deed; Mark shows how Jesus nourished and strengthened Jairus's faith in him.

Note that Jairus was one of the rulers of the synagogue. These were laymen who took care of the administrative duties at the synagogue, somewhat like the members of a church council today. They were prominent men, but most of them, as we shall see, were opposed to Christ and did not believe in him. However this ruler in his hour of need sought out Christ, forgot his dignity and fell on his knees before the

Lord with a petition. Love for his daughter sent him to Christ, for he realized that only Christ could help her. Jesus did not reject Jairus. (All who come to him are welcome.) But true faith in Jesus had to come not only from concern and need; it had to recognize him for what he truly was —not just a healer, but the Son of God become man. And Jairus was about to be taught that by means of an interruption on the way to his house.

A Woman with a Hemorrhage Healed

A large crowd followed Jesus, and he was pressed from all sides. And then came a touch that Jesus immediately recognized as totally different, a touch of faith pleading for help. It was a woman who for twelve years had suffered from hemorrhages, had consulted all the doctors available but had found no help. In fact, her condition was worse now than in the beginning. Also, she had spent all her funds — doctors' bills were just as high then as now. But she had heard about Jesus, and what she had heard had kindled faith in her heart that he would also be able to help her. If we restrict this to what Mark has already told, she had perhaps heard about the leper and the paralytic who had been healed. She was therefore sure that there would be help for her too.

Her condition embarrassed her. If it was a menstrual hemorrhage, it had made her unclean ceremonially and had kept her out of the temple and the synagogue. She was shunned by all who knew her condition — a lonesome, sick, poor woman — but no longer hopeless! Not willing to make a public request for help, she said, to herself, "I will just touch his clothes," and promptly did so. She was healed instantly and felt it in her body.

But Jesus knew too. He realized power had gone out from him. And he knew who was healed. His asking and looking around were simply meant to bring her forward, to correct his disciples and to support her in her faith. The KJV gives a more accurate translation of verse 32 than the NIV: "And he looked round about to see *her* that had done this thing." With fear and trembling she came forward and told him everything. Was she afraid that he would undo the miracle or chastise her for not observing the Levitical law?

We don't know what was going on in her mind, but we do know the words of Jesus. He called her "daughter," a word of loving concern, though she may have been older than Jesus. And then he said, "Your faith has healed you"; that is, your faith in my ability and willingness to heal you has brought you healing from me. His next words, "Be freed from your suffering," assured her that her healing wasn't a dream on her part; her suffering would never return. And if she told Jesus that she had been ill twelve years (remember, she "told him the whole truth"), that really must have startled Jairus, since his daughter was twelve years old. How it must have strengthened his faith to see Jesus perform this miracle! Undoubtedly that's a reason Jesus had this woman give her testimony.

Jairus's Daughter Raised from the Dead

At this point Jairus's faith was really put to the test. Men came from his house and told him his daughter was dead. That was crushing news — so final! Certainly Jesus could do nothing about death! Their following advice — "Why bother the teacher any more?" — was logical, just as the words of the disciples in verse 31 had been. And it would have been true, if Jesus had been only a teacher. But Mark in the opening words of his Gospel declared that Jesus Christ is the Son of God. Up to this point the miracle about to follow will have been the most convincing proof of that.

Before Jairus could say a word, perhaps to say he was sorry he had bothered Christ, Jesus exclaimed, "Don't be afraid; just believe." The anguished father put his faith in Jesus and followed him home. Jesus dismissed the crowd, for they undoubtedly were looking upon him more as a healer than the promised Savior, but took Peter, James and John along as his witnesses. From here on they would be special witnesses of Christ in a number of other instances, when more would have been a crowd, but one would not have been enough (see 2 Corinthians 13:1).

Was the girl actually dead? The evidence is clear. When Jesus and his three disciples and Jairus came to the home, the professional mourners had already been summoned. Burial usually was on the day of death or the following morning. Those who were there knew she was dead. When Jesus said, "The child is not dead but asleep," they laughed at him. They knew better.

In the presence of the power of God, however, death was no more than a sleep, as the child's father and mother and the three disciples of Jesus were about to discover. Jesus took the dead girl by the hand and said, "*Talitha koum!*" Immediately she stood up and walked about.

Mark records the actual Aramaic words spoken by Jesus. Thus we hear the life-giving syllables Mark had so often heard from the lips of Peter, an eyewitness. Jesus is indeed the Lord of life and death.

How often later the parents must have told the girl about what Jesus had done for her. The crowds and the professional mourners had not been permitted to witness the miracle. Jesus had ordered the parents not to tell others. Yet the very presence of the girl could not keep the miracle a secret.

Jesus also cared. He called her "little girl," just as Jairus had called her "my little daughter " He told her parents to give her something to eat. In their amazement they just hadn't thought that far. Jesus knew that after her illness her body needed nourishment. Completely well, she lived an ordinary life again. She needed food and clothing and all the other things her parents could and would provide for her.

This is a miracle we also need to look at and take its meaning to heart. Unless we live until judgment day, we too will die. Loved ones, acquaintances and past generations have all gone that way. But death is not the end. The eternal Son of God has conquered death not only for Jairus's daugther, but also for you and me, for he has paid for the sins of all. He died our death and has promised to raise us up again on the last day. Our death too will be but a sleep. Awakening from it through his word of power, we shall live with him forever. And remember, Christ did not do this in secret. There were five witnesses, three of whom were his disciples who later went out and proclaimed him as the Lord of life. This miracle proclaims his deity and assures us of our salvation.

A Prophet Without Honor

6 **Jesus left there and went to his hometown, accompanied by his disciples. [2]When the Sabbath came, he began to teach in the synagogue, and many who heard him were amazed.**

"Where did this man get these things?" they asked. "What's this wisdom that has been given him, that he even does miracles! [3]Isn't this the carpenter? Isn't this Mary's son and the brother of James, Joseph, Judas and Simon? Aren't his sisters here with us?" And they took offense at him.

[4]Jesus said to them, "Only in his hometown, among his relatives and in his own house is a prophet without honor." [5]He could not do any miracles there, except lay his hands on a few sick people and heal them. [6]And he was amazed at their lack of faith.
(Matthew 13:54-58; Luke 4:16-30)

Mark does not dwell on the message Jesus proclaimed, but on the hostile reaction of Jesus' hearers. Mark's account is almost identical with that of Matthew. Luke tells us in some detail what Jesus preached in the synagogue that Sabbath when he pointed to himself as the promised Savior.

Accompanied by his disciples, Jesus came to his hometown Nazareth as a rabbi, a teacher. It was not a family visit. This synagogue Jesus had attended as a boy, a teenager and a young man. The worshipers that day were all people who knew him well. He had now come to share the gospel with them, but they were not ready to receive him as the one who embodied the gospel. In a certain sense this incident was important training for the disciples, who shortly would be proclaiming the gospel themselves and also facing rebuffs. They could say, "They did the same to our Master."

The synagogue audience was amazed at Jesus' teaching and at his miracles of which they had heard. In their eyes he was no more than a carpenter, a son of Mary, one who had four brothers and whose sisters were married and living in Nazareth. He was one of them, just an ordinary fellow who once made his living with his hands. How could he claim to be a prophet and the fulfillment of Scripture? It was more than they could stomach. They rejected his claim and then in their wrath attempted to cast him off the cliff at the edge of town (see Luke 4:28-30). Since the day ended with an attempt on Jesus' life, the healings mentioned in verse five undoubtedly were performed before the Sabbath synagogue service, perhaps on Friday. But even then there were only a few who brought their sick to him. Apathy and unbelief filled the whole town. Since these were people who had studied their Old Testament in the synagogue, even as Jesus had when living among them, it is not surprising that our Lord "was amazed at their lack of faith." Knowing the Scriptures, they were without excuse in refusing to acknowledge him as God's prophet and their Savior.

Before leaving this dark day in the life of our Lord, we must call attention to a few other facts which Mark has brought to our attention. Four of Jesus' brothers were mentioned as well as his sisters. Who were they? There is no reason to believe they were anything but children of Mary and Joseph born after the virgin birth of Jesus. In contrast to the sisters, the brothers seemed to be no longer living in Nazareth. In Mark we have met them once before in Capernaum (3:31-35) where Jesus had moved his family after the wedding in Cana of Galilee. It was not until after the resurrection of Jesus that his brothers became believers.

What happened to Christ in Nazareth can also happen to us. Just because we are followers of the Lord does not guarantee that all our relatives, neighbors and acquaintances will welcome the gospel message — or even our children. At times some of us stand alone, ridiculed and mocked by those who know us best. But it is easier to bear when we realize Jesus also had to bear that same burden.

Jesus' Ministry in Galilee and the Regions Beyond Draws to a Close
Jesus Sends Out the Twelve

⁶Then Jesus went around teaching from village to village. ⁷Calling the Twelve to him, he sent them out two by two and gave them authority over evil spirits.

⁸These were his instructions: "Take nothing for the journey except a staff — no bread, no bag, no money in your belts. ⁹Wear sandals but not an extra tunic. ¹⁰Whenever you enter a house, stay there until you leave that town. ¹¹And if any place will not welcome you or listen to you, shake the dust off your feet when you leave, as a testimony against them."

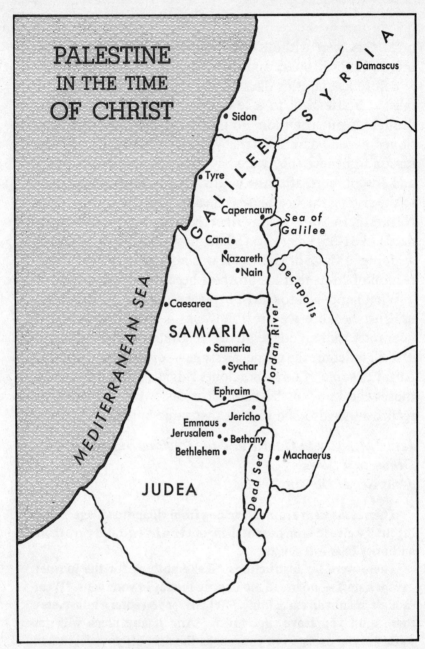

Palestine in the Time of Christ

¹²**They went out and preached that people should repent.**
¹³**They drove out many demons and anointed many sick people
with oil and healed them.**
(Matthew 10:5—11:1; Luke 9:1-6)

The rejection Jesus experienced at Nazareth did not keep
him from continuing his gospel ministry. Disappointed and
grieved as he was, he continued to travel the preaching
circuit from one village to another. And then he took another step, that of sending the Twelve out two by two on their
own preaching tour in Galilee.

Why? There undoubtedly were a number of reasons. One,
because the time was growing short to get the message out
into all the villages of the "lost sheep of Israel" (Matthew
10:5,6). Another, remember the Lord had said to Peter and
Andrew, "I will make you fishers of men." To do so, he had
to train his disciples. What better way was there to do this
than to give them personal experience? This preaching tour
was for them what the vicar or intern experience is for
seminary students today as they prepare to become ministers of Christ.

Why two by two? One reason is suggested by Deuteronomy 17:6, where in serious cases (those involving the death
penalty) no decision was to be made based only on the
testimony of one witness. Here it was also a matter of life or
death — eternal life or eternal death! Undoubtedly there
was also a practical reason. When meeting those who would
oppose them, two would be better than one because of the
support they could offer one another.

Today we would not think of sending one missionary all
by himself into a foreign mission field. There is need for
missionaries also to serve one another with the word and to
supplement each other's knowledge when facing difficult
problems. The Lord's apostles were no different. Acts re-

cords how Paul also always took one or more helpers with him wherever he went.

Another question: Why give the apostles authority over evil spirits? Because the apostles were Christ's official delegates. Their hearers would not accept them as the representatives of Christ unless they had the same ability to drive out demons that Christ had so often demonstrated. A case in point is the account in Mark 9:14-29. The words of Paul in 2 Corinthians 12:12, "The things that mark an apostle — signs, wonders and miracles — were done among you with great perseverance," speak of marks of the apostles.

Surprising were Christ's directives to his disciples in preparing them for this preaching mission. They were to take nothing along but a staff, an aid in walking the many miles, but no other provisions — no bread, no bag (supplies) and no money. They were to wear sandals, but only one tunic, unlike other travelers who usually took an extra one to cover up with at night. Jesus thus assured them their needs would be met and they would always have a warm place to sleep. After all, by his own preaching and teaching in the various places he had prepared the way for them.

Does this mean that when we today call pastors or commission missionaries, this is what we should expect of them too? Not at all. We are to use normal prudence. Note that in Luke 22:35-37 Christ changed his instructions for those who would carry on his work after his death, resurrection and ascension. They would by no means always be welcomed and so would have to be able to take care of their needs. Today this obligation is laid upon the congregations and church bodies. See the directives in 1 Timothy 5:17,18.

Then why not this time? In order to build up their reliance on their Lord and Master. On this training tour they were to learn the truth of what he would tell them later, "Surely I am with you always" (Matthew 28:20), and thus be prepared to face situations such as those recorded in Mark 13:11: "Whenever you are arrested and brought to trial, do not worry beforehand about what to say. Just say whatever is given you at the time, for it is not you speaking, but the Holy Spirit." No matter what our situation, every pastor, teacher and lay Christian still needs Christ, even as Paul learned in his troubles (see 2 Corinthians 11).

The Lord also included an admonition. The disciples were to accept the hospitality offered them. They were not in it for what they could get out of it. The Lord did not hide from them that not all would welcome them, no more than he was welcomed at Nazareth. He told them that in such a case they were to "shake the dust off your feet as a testimony against them" — a testimony against them on the day of judgment (Matthew 11:21-24) or, pray God, a judging that would finally lead them to recognize their sins and thus lead them to repentance.

The disciples did as Jesus directed. It was a successful preaching tour. Their message was supported by their driving out demons and healing the sick.

What about the oil they used in connection with the healings? Does this mean the church is to use oil in a service of healing? Does this passage support the Roman Catholic "sacrament of extreme unction"? Note that there is no command on the part of our Lord to use oil. The disciples' use of oil was a customary practice — to soothe the patient. It is not presented here as being responsible for the cure. The disciples healed the sick in the name of Jesus. Nor is this the "sacrament of extreme unction," although this passage is used as evidence by the Roman Church. The use of oil has absolutely nothing to do with preparation for death. That it brings the forgiveness of sins is likewise a misrepresentation of James 5:14,15.

There are some seeming contradictions here. Mark reports Jesus as saying, "Take nothing for the journey except a staff — no bread, no bag, no money in your belts. Wear sandals but not an extra tunic." Luke 9:3 states: "Take nothing for the journey — no staff, no bag, no bread, no money, no extra tunic." Matthew 10:9,10 records: "Do not take along any gold or silver or copper in your belts; take no bag for the journey, or extra tunic, or sandals or a staff."

There are differences in these accounts, aren't there? Are they contradictions? A careful reading will indicate that Mark says, "Wear sandals," but that Matthew does not say, "Wear no sandals," but "take no sandals" along, that is, no extra pair. Mark says, "Take nothing ... except a staff," and Luke says, "Take nothing for the journey — no staff." Luke puts this with the "no" list of things to be taken in addition to the necessities like sandals on the feet, a tunic to cover the body, and a staff in the hand to aid in walking. In other words: "Go as you are. Don't pack extras. Yes, the staff you have is necessary."

The Gospels, if read closely, do not contradict one another; they supplement one another. The same is true when the Gospel writers at times place events in a different order. They have a reason for introducing them at a specific point, and we ought to study their words to learn what that is. The evangelists are not writing a biography of our Lord's life. They were introducing him to us so that we may learn to know him through his acts and through his words. John particularly complements the other three and fills in many a gap. Let's not look for errors where there are none.

John the Baptist Beheaded

14King Herod heard about this, for Jesus' name had become well known. Some were saying, "John the Baptist has been raised from the dead, and that is why miraculous powers are at work in him."

¹⁵Others said, "He is Elijah."

And still others claimed, "He is a prophet, like one of the prophets of long ago."

¹⁶But when Herod heard this, he said, "John, the man I beheaded, has been raised from the dead!"

¹⁷For Herod himself had given orders to have John arrested and he had him bound and put in prison. He did this because of Herodias, his brother Philip's wife, whom he had married. ¹⁸For John had been saying to Herod, "It is not lawful for you to have your brother's wife." ¹⁹So Herodias nursed a grudge against John and wanted to kill him. But she was not able to, ²⁰because Herod feared John and protected him, knowing him to be a righteous and holy man. When Herod heard John, he was greatly puzzled; yet he liked to listen to him.

²¹Finally the opportune time came. On his birthday Herod gave a banquet for his high officials and military commanders and the leading men of Galilee. ²²When the daughter of Herodias came in and danced, she pleased Herod and his dinner guests.

The king said to the girl, "Ask me for anything you want, and I'll give it to you." ²³And he promised her with an oath, "Whatever you ask I will give you, up to half of my kingdom."

²⁴She went out and said to her mother, "What shall I ask for?"

"The head of John the Baptist," she answered.

²⁵At once the girl hurried in to the king with the request: "I want you to give me right now the head of John the Baptist on a platter."

²⁶The king was greatly distressed, but because of his oaths and his dinner guests, he did not want to refuse her. ²⁷So he immediately sent an executioner with orders to bring John's head. The man went, beheaded John in prison, ²⁸and brought back his head on a platter. He presented it to the girl, and she gave it to her mother. ²⁹On hearing of this, John's disciples came and took his body and laid it in a tomb.

(Matthew 14:1-12; Luke 9:7-9)

The increased activity of our Lord, his sending the apostles out on preaching missions, did not remain unnoticed. When King Herod heard about it, he was reminded of John's activities. In fact, he was convinced that Jesus was John "raised from the dead."

The story of Herod and Herodias had all the earmarks of a TV soap opera, only it was real life. A brief review of history will help us understand Herodias's hatred for John. Herod Antipas was the son of Herod the Great, who ruled at the time of Jesus' birth. His mother was Malthace, one of ten women who at some time or other were wives of Herod the Great. Herod Antipas, popularly known as king, was actually a tetrarch and ruled over Galilee and Perea from 4 B.C. to A.D. 39. His first wife was the daughter of Aretas IV, ruler of Nabataea, an Arab kingdom southeast of Palestine having its capital at Petra. Aretas is mentioned again in 2 Corinthians 11:32 and at that time seems to have had control of Damascus as well. In A.D. 27 Herod Antipas visited Rome and there met the beautiful and ambitious Herodias, daughter of his half-brother Aristobulus (thus his niece) who was then married to another of his half-brothers, Herod Philip. They deserted their spouses and married, though related in a degree forbidden in Leviticus 18:16 and 20:21. The first wife of Antipas upon hearing about it fled back to her father's court, and that later led to a war in which Herod was soundly defeated in A.D. 36. Herod's marital escapade became the talk of the entire region. John the Baptist also censured the incestuous relationship. This enraged Herodias and led to John's imprisonment and to his murder. How often murder and adultery go together!

When Herod heard of Jesus' activity and that of his disciples, he was convinced the only explanation was that John had been brought back to life. Not only Herod thought so, but many others also. That's how they explained the miracles done by Christ and his apostles. Note, they did not deny the resurrection.

When John had originally appeared preaching and baptizing, priests and Levites from Jerusalem, mindful of the prophecy in Malachi 4:5,6, had questioned John. They asked whether he was the promised Messiah or Elijah or one of the other prophets. John denied being any of them and stated that he was the one sent to prepare the way for the Messiah. But the rumors did not stop, and, when he died and Jesus' activity increased, the people began to identify Jesus as John brought back to life, as Elijah, as the prophet of Deuteronomy 18:15, or as one of the other prophets. (See Mark 8:27,28). Though all this fell short of reality, it testifies to the impression Christ made on those who heard him or heard about him. Herod's reaction was dictated by an evil conscience.

At this point Mark records what happened to John some time before this in the fortress of Machaerus near the Dead Sea. Herod had imprisoned John to satisfy his "wife's" demands. Herod at first also wanted to kill John but feared to do so, because he knew John to be a righteous and holy man (see Matthew 14:5). Strange as it may seem, Herod liked to listen to John, although he was "greatly puzzled," something to be expected of a man who had violated everything God had ordered in the Old Testament. This explains why John's imprisonment was less harsh than usual; Matthew 11:2 and Luke 7:19 record that his disciples were permitted to visit him. This, however, infuriated Herodias.

Finally her chance for revenge came, and her planning paid off. At the banquet marking Herod's birthday, Salome, the daughter of Herodias by her first marriage, danced for Herod and his guests. That they enjoyed it doesn't say much for the morals of the leading men of Galilee. Herod's oath

—an oath in uncertain things — should also have offended them, for it was anything but proper and God-pleasing. But not a one spoke up.

After her dance and Herod's promise with an oath, Salome immediately consulted her mother. Then she asked for the head of John the Baptist "right now" and "on a platter." Like mother, like daughter — no conscience whatsoever. But the most tragic character in this soap opera-like affair was Herod. Distressed, yes! But his pride did not permit him to recant his oath. He feared men more than God. What a warning for us who read it!

And John? He had no time to prepare for death. In walked the soldier, and off came John's head. But he was prepared; he knew his Savior. While in prison, when his mind once raised questions, he sent his disciples to Christ and received the answer his heart needed (see Matthew 11:2-15). He died trusting and believing in the Savior whose way he had prepared. No wonder Jesus spoke of him as "the Elijah who was to come." Though John died when about thirty-three, we need not feel sorry for him. It is Herod, Herodias, Salome and the guests at the banquet whom we feel sorry for. Later, in Holy Week, Herod had the opportunity of questioning Christ personally, but his record then was no better than it was with John. He became a friend of Pilate, but not a follower of Jesus Christ.

The disciples of John, clearly with Herod's permission, came and took the body and buried it. What a day of sadness and grief! But these disciples had taken the preaching of John to heart, for they came and told Jesus (see Matthew 14:12). For our Lord it was an indication of what was about to face him and that time was running out.

Jesus Feeds the Five Thousand

³⁰The apostles gathered around Jesus and reported to him all they had done and taught. ³¹Then, because so many people were coming and going that they did not even have a chance to eat, he said to them, "Come with me by yourselves to a quiet place and get some rest."

³²So they went away by themselves in a boat to a solitary place. ³³But many who saw them leaving recognized them and ran on foot from all the towns and got there ahead of them. ³⁴When Jesus landed and saw a large crowd, he had compassion on them, because they were like sheep without a shepherd. So he began teaching them many things.

³⁵By this time it was late in the day, so his disciples came to him. "This is a remote place," they said, "and it's already very late. ³⁶Send the people away so they can go to the surrounding countryside and villages and buy themselves something to eat."

³⁷But he answered, "You give them something to eat."

They said to him, "That would take eight months of a man's wages! Are we to go and spend that much on bread and give it to them to eat?"

³⁸"How many loaves do you have?" he asked. "Go and see."

When they found out, they said, "Five — and two fish."

³⁹Then Jesus directed them to have all the people sit down in groups on the green grass. ⁴⁰So they sat down in groups of hundreds and fifties. ⁴¹Taking the five loaves and the two fish and looking up to heaven, he gave thanks and broke the loaves. Then he gave them to his disciples to set before the people. He also divided the two fish among them all. ⁴²They all ate and were satisfied, ⁴³and the disciples picked up twelve basketfuls of broken pieces of bread and fish. ⁴⁴The number of the men who had eaten was five thousand.

(Matthew 14:13-21; Luke 9:10-17; John 6:1-15)

Mark again takes up the account of the sending out of the Twelve. He properly calls them apostles, the Greek word that designates them as such who had been commissioned and sent out on a mission. Just how long they had been gone is not stated. We may assume that Jesus had set a definite time for them to return. The reports they brought back must have been exciting, but perhaps not all necessarily good, since otherwise Jesus would not have warned them in advance what to do in case their message was not accepted (6:11).

Whenever Jesus was in Capernaum, people simply did not leave him alone. This time Jesus and his disciples did not even find time to eat, to say nothing about being able to discuss the disciples' missionary journey in detail. Rest was also needed after their strenuous tour. God's servants today need to set aside periods of rest and meditation, and missionaries need furloughs for time with their families and friends stateside.

Jesus therefore suggested some privacy and rest. Jesus and his disciples left by boat, but their effort at privacy was futile. Noting the direction the boat went, the people headed for the same area on foot and in fact even arrived ahead of Jesus and his disciples. When they landed, according to John 6, Jesus and his disciples withdrew for a while to a hillside. But our Lord could not resist meeting the needs of the multitude and soon was in their midst preaching and teaching. He knew that they were sheep without a shepherd. In their synagogues, as recorded in the beginning of this chapter, they were not given the spiritual food they needed and were not directed to the promised Messiah. Christ, the Shepherd who could provide them with what they needed, could not withhold the food they so desperately desired.

The day passed quickly, and soon it was late afternoon. This gave Jesus an opportunity to test his apostles to see whether they had learned a lesson on their mission tour. Concerned that the people had not eaten, the apostles came to Jesus with a very practical suggestion. They asked him to send the people away so that they could buy the necessary food in the neighboring villages and, according to Luke, also find lodging. The apostles could hardly believe their ears when Jesus told them to feed the crowd themselves. Why, even eight months' wages would not buy sufficient to give all of them a little! The apostles had forgotten how Jesus in sending them out had assured them that they would be provided for (6:8-10). But before we criticize them, let's ask whether we would have given any better account of ourselves!

Then Jesus took over. The food available amounted to five loaves and two small fish which, according to John 6:8, belonged to a young lad. A barley loaf was flat and small, hardly enough for two people, and the fish, pickled or smoked, usually served as relish or garnish and was eaten with the bread. Not much to go on. But the disciples seemed to have caught on that something special was in the wind when Jesus asked them to seat the people, for they did so without raising any more questions.

The sight must have been stunning — a large crowd grouped by fifties and hundreds seated on the green grass. The word "group" in Greek is the word used for beds in a garden, orderly rows of vegetables. All sat there waiting to be fed by their Good Shepherd, but totally unaware of what was about to happen.

Jesus began this meal, as he began every other meal, by giving thanks. It was the usual blessing, but an unusual meal. Now if our Lord regularly gave thanks, shouldn't we also give thanks when we receive from him what meets the needs of our body?

Jesus broke the loaves and divided the fish. Then without saying a word he simply continued to multiply the bread and

fish, so that there was enough for all and even more left over
— twelve baskets, one for each one of the doubting disciples
— than they had started with. And don't forget that more
than 5,000 had eaten, counting the women and children.

What does this miracle teach us about Christ? It is clear
that he is more than just a man; he is also God, for what he
did was a creative act. If Christ did that here and then again
when he fed the 4,000, why should anyone doubt that he is
able to give us his body and blood again and again in the
Lord's Supper as he has promised?

John 6:14,15 informs us about the effect Jesus' miracle
had on the people. They saw in his action a fulfillment of Old
Testament prophecies and immediately wanted to make him
king by force. However they had not understood their Old
Testament correctly. What they desired to do would have
destroyed everything that Christ had been sent to accomplish. Thus this was another of Satan's temptations (see
Luke 4:13), but again one Jesus did not fall for.

Jesus Walks on the Water

⁴⁵Immediately Jesus made his disciples get into the boat and go
ahead of him to Bethsaida, while he dismissed the crowd. ⁴⁶After
leaving them, he went up on a mountainside to pray.

⁴⁷When evening came, the boat was in the middle of the lake,
and he was alone on land. ⁴⁸He saw the disciples straining at the
oars, because the wind was against them. About the fourth watch
of the night he went out to them, walking on the lake. He was
about to pass by them, ⁴⁹but when they saw him walking on the
lake, they thought he was a ghost. They cried out, ⁵⁰because they
all saw him and were terrified.

Immediately he spoke to them and said, "Take courage! It is I.
Don't be afraid." ⁵¹Then he climbed into the boat with them, and
the wind died down. They were completely amazed, ⁵²for they had
not understood about the loaves; their hearts were hardened.
(Matthew 14:22-33; John 6:16-21)

Jesus dismissed the people and immediately ordered his disciples to go by boat to Bethsaida. This suggests that perhaps the disciples themselves had been inclined to join the crowd in its efforts to proclaim Jesus king. Jesus then withdrew into the hills to pray, as he did so frequently when facing a criticial hour.

When night fell, the disciples were in the middle of the lake and completely off course because they were facing a strong head wind. It was so contrary that they had taken down the sail and picked up the oars. And even that had brought them nowhere on the stormy lake. They were in real danger.

Jesus though deep in prayer was aware of their situation. He let them struggle for some time in order to show them, as he so often shows us, that he is able to help in the hour of need. In the fourth watch of the night (between 3:00 and 6:00 A.M.) Jesus went to help them. The winds and the waves did not hinder our Lord as he walked on the water. When approaching the ship, he walked as though he would pass by. This was by design — to get the attention of the disciples and to test them. What happened does not say much for them. Superstition overwhelmed them. They were terrified and imagined they saw a ghost. Undoubtedly we would have reacted in much the same way. Jesus' words calmed their fears, as he assured them that it was truly he.

Mark concentrates on Jesus' miracles, his walking on the water and controlling the wind so that it died down the moment Jesus entered the ship. John adds that the boat immediately reached the shore. When we ponder these miracles, we cannot doubt that Christ is the Lord of creation. Mark does not have the details Matthew adds that show how Peter's faith failed and how Jesus had to rescue him, nor that when Jesus entered the boat the disciples worshiped him, saying, "Truly you are the Son of God."

Despite their confession they did not fully understand what had taken place. Mark stresses that by saying if they had fully understood the feeding of the 5,000, they would have been prepared for this miracle too. The statement that their hearts were hardened does not mean they rejected Christ or did not believe in him as their Savior, but that they failed to grasp fully what he had done. Their hearts were not open to what Jesus was seeking to teach them. Mark is very candid about exposing the spiritual weaknesses of the disciples and very lucid in expounding the greatness of Christ.

That Jesus' walking on the water really took place and is not just a story or myth (as some say) is evident. Mark clearly states, "They all saw him." He wasn't seen by just one or two, but not by the others. We thank the Holy Spirit for moving Mark to bring out this fact.

Jesus Is Constantly Followed by Crowds

53When they had crossed over, they landed at Gennesaret and anchored there. 54As soon as they got out of the boat, people recognized Jesus. 55They ran throughout that whole region and carried the sick on mats to wherever they heard he was. 56And everywhere he went — into villages, towns or countryside — they placed the sick in the marketplaces. They begged him to let them touch even the edge of his cloak, and all who touched him were healed.

(Matthew 14:34-36)

It is from John's Gospel that we learn when Jesus and his disciples landed in the area of Gennesaret, they set out for nearby Capernaum, where Jesus on the following day gave his discourse on the bread of life (Christ himself). After hearing these words, many of his followers began leaving him. It seems they were ready to settle for earthly bread, but not for the spiritual food Christ offered them when he pointed to himself as the only way to the Father.

In the meantime those who had recognized Christ as he stepped off the boat at Gennesaret immediately went throughout the region with the news that Jesus was in the area. Crowds welcomed him in the days that followed as he went through villages, towns and countryside. Wherever he came, they brought their sick to him for healing. Jesus was even willing to heal those who in faith touched the edge of his cloak (see Matthew 9:20-22 and Mark 5:27-34).

Thus Mark again shows us the divine power of our Lord even as he did in Jesus' feeding of the 5,000 and walking on the water. Though Mark does not mention it, Jesus undoubtedly also used these occasions to proclaim the gospel of the kingdom, the spiritual healing his hearers needed even more than the physical healing.

Commandments of God and Traditions of Men

7 The Pharisees and some of the teachers of the law who had come from Jerusalem gathered around Jesus and ²saw some of his disciples eating food with hands that were "unclean," that is, unwashed. ³(The Pharisees and all the Jews do not eat unless they give their hands a ceremonial washing, holding to the tradition of the elders. ⁴When they come from the marketplace they do not eat unless they wash. And they observe many other traditions, such as the washing of cups, pitchers and kettles.)

⁵So the Pharisees and teachers of the law asked Jesus, "Why don't your disciples live according to the tradition of the elders instead of eating their food with 'unclean' hands?"

⁶He replied, "Isaiah was right when he prophesied about you hypocrites; as it is written:

'These people honor me with their lips,
but their hearts are far from me.
⁷They worship me in vain;
their teachings are but rules taught by men.'

[8] You have let go of the commands of God and are holding on to the traditions of men."

And he said to them: "You have a fine way of setting aside the commands of God in order to observe your own traditions! [10] For Moses said, 'Honor your father and your mother,' and 'Anyone who curses his father or mother must be put to death.' [11] But you say that if a man says to his father or mother: 'Whatever help you might otherwise have received from me is Corban' (that is, a gift devoted to God), [12] then you no longer let him do anything for his father or mother. [13] Thus you nullify the word of God by your tradition that you have handed down. And you do many things like that."

[14] Again Jesus called the crowd to him and said, "Listen to me, everyone, and understand this. [15] Nothing outside a man can make him 'unclean' by going into him. Rather, it is what comes out of a man that makes him 'unclean.' "

[17] After he had left the crowd and entered the house, his disciples asked him about this parable. [18] "Are you so dull?" he asked. "Don't you see that nothing that enters a man from the outside can make him 'unclean'? [19] For it doesn't go into his heart but into his stomach, and then out of his body" (In saying this, Jesus declared all foods "clean.")

[20] He went on: "What comes out of a man is what makes him 'unclean.' [21] For from within, out of men's hearts, come evil thoughts, sexual immorality, theft, murder, adultery, [22] greed, malice, deceit, lewdness, envy, slander, arrogance and folly. [23] All these evils come from inside and make a man 'unclean.' "

(Matthew 15:1-11,15-20)

It almost seems as though the Pharisees and the teachers of the law, the theologians of that day, had a point in criticizing Jesus. Their real target, after all, was Christ, not the disciples. At first glance, it seems as though Jesus was indeed ignoring the ceremonial laws God had given by not rebuking his disciples for eating with unwashed hands. Not so. Then what is the situation?

When God created man and woman, he placed his moral law into their hearts so that they might conduct their lives as obedient children of God. Unfortunately they sinned, and death is the wages of sin. The only solution was the one God provided. He promised the Savior who would pay for their sins and fully keep the law in their place. In order that this promise might be fulfilled, God chose the descendants of Abraham, Isaac and Jacob as the nation from which the Savior would be born. To make sure that they would remain separate from all other nations, God repeated his will in the Ten Commandments and then gave them numerous ceremonial laws that would set them apart from the other nations.

Israel, as the years passed, ignored God's word more and more. Many forgot the promise and zeroed in on the commandments of God as the way to heaven. Still there were always such who clung to the promise and recognized the commandments as a way to safeguard the existence of the gospel promise. Later, during the fourth and third centuries before the birth of Christ, there were those who considered the moral law and the ceremonial laws God had given them as insufficient. So they augmented them and finally came up with 613 rules regulating Israel's life down to the smallest details. The gospel promise was ignored, and salvation became something to be earned by one's own righteousness. Again, not by all, as we learn from Anna the prophetess, who after Jesus was presented in the temple "spoke about the child to all who were looking forward to the redemption of Jerusalem" (Luke 2:38).

Among these ceremonial regulations were the ones Mark here mentioned. Mark went into detail because his first readers were Gentiles, unacquainted with many of these matters. What Jesus (and Mark, the writer of this Gospel) was concerned about was that these expansions of the Old

Testament ceremonial laws did not have God's backing. In fact, at times they abrogated God's own moral law.

God's moral law still stands. We know, of course, that it cannot save us. Only Christ and his gospel can do that. The Old Testament ceremonial laws, however, no longer apply today. The Father himself indicated that when at the death of Christ on Calvary he caused the curtain in the temple to be "torn in two from top to bottom" (15:38), thus opening free access to God. That's why Paul in Colossians 2:17 says that the ceremonial laws "are a shadow of the things that were to come, the reality, however, is found in Christ." Philippians 3:3 assures us New Testament believers: "It is we who are the circumcision, we who worship by the Spirit of God, who glory in Christ Jesus, and who put no confidence in the flesh."

The Pharisees and teachers of the law mentioned in this portion of Mark did put their confidence in the flesh. What is more, they did so in a way that made them hypocrites and demolishers of God's own word. They reduced the ceremonial commands of the Scripture and their own traditions to outward acts they could perform without actually involving the heart. That's why Jesus applied the words of Isaiah 29:13 to them: "These people come near to me with their mouth and honor me with their lips, but their hearts are far from me. Their worship of me is made up only of rules taught by men." What a tragic loss when we remember that God's Old Testament ceremonial laws were meant to prepare the way for Christ!

What's worse, their teachings also at times undermined the moral law. Christ pointed out how they violated the Fourth Commandment. They permitted children to refuse help to needy parents by simply calling what they needed for help "Corban," that is, a gift dedicated to God or promised to the temple. Jesus in this connection told them exactly what they did: "You nullify the word of God."

The Judaism of Jesus' day, as well as the Judaism of our own day (though we understand it has modified some of the extreme forms of "Corban"), needed these penetrating words of Jesus. The disciples later told Jesus, "Do you know that the Pharisees were offended when they heard this?" (Matthew 15:12). Let's hope that for at least some of them that was the first step in the right direction.

What Jesus told these Pharisees and teachers of the law, he also shared with the people and with his disciples. This was necessary, since all of them had been brought up to honor and respect the Pharisees and teachers of the law, but were not aware of how their teaching had undermined the main thrust of the Old Testament, the promise of the coming Savior and salvation only through him. Because of this we also need these words of Christ.

It isn't food in itself, Jesus told them, that is unclean, including even the food forbidden by the Old Testament ceremonial laws. Food after all goes into the stomach and passes out of the body. It is what comes out of the heart in violation of God's commandments — and for Old Testament Israel that included the ceremonial laws, though it does not do so for us — that is the unclean element. The list (vv 21-23) is a comprehensive one and is also an accurate picture of society's actions in our own day. And since we have an old Adam, we too need to take Jesus' words to heart. They prove we cannot save ourselves; he alone can do that. In gratitude to him we want to avoid these unclean acts, words, thoughts and desires that are a part of our inborn nature, and with his help fight against them.

The Greek word used for the "washing" of cups, pitchers and kettles (v 4) is the word "baptize." There are those who insist this word means "immerse," and therefore immersion is the only proper mode of baptism. Here the Greek manuscript used by the King James Version is instructive. It reads: "the washing of cups, and pots, brazen vessels, and of tables." Cups, pots and brazen vessels can be immersed, but not tables. Thus the Greek word for baptism cannot mean only "immerse." To insist that it does is to become modern day "Pharisees and teachers of the law," who nullify the word of God by their own traditions. Let us cling to the freedom Christ has won for us.

The Faith of a Syrophenician Woman

24Jesus left that place and went to the vicinity of Tyre. He entered a house and did not want anyone to know it; yet he could not keep his presence secret. 254In fact, as soon as she heard about him, a woman whose little daughter was possessed by an evil spirit came and fell at his feet. 26The woman was a Greek, born in Syrian Phoenicia. She begged Jesus to drive the demon out of her daughter.

27"First let the children eat all they want," he told her, "for it is not right to take the children's bread and toss it to their dogs."

28"Yes, Lord," she replied, "but even the dogs under the table eat the children's crumbs."

29Then he told her, "For such a relpy, you may go; the demon has left your daughter."

30She went home and found her child lying on the bed, and the demon gone.

(Matthew 15:21-28)

People simply gave the Lord no privacy. If it wasn't the 5,000, it was the Pharisees and the teachers of the law, or such who needed healing. There was no time to instruct his disciples. This finally forced Jesus to take the unusual step of leaving Israelite territory and of entering Gentile territory in the vicinity of Tyre and Sidon, today known as Lebanon.

But even there Jesus could not keep his presence a secret — thirteen men are quite a group. So almost immediately a Gentile woman approached him and begged him to help her daughter, who was possessed by an evil spirit. Her actions and her words show she believed he was able to help. Undoubtedly she had heard what he had done in Israel.

This caused a predicament for our Lord. He had been sent to fulfill the promises given by God to Israel. To begin a preaching and healing tour through Gentile territory could have delayed, perhaps even undermined, God's plan of redemption. Still there was this great need, and he was the only one who could help. This explains Jesus' words about the children's bread being tossed to their "dogs."

Jesus' words seemed harsh. The Israelites often called the Gentiles "dogs," meaning scavengers and animals. However the Greek word here used — and Christ seems to have been speaking in Greek to this woman — means "pet dogs" or "puppies." The woman understood Jesus' reply in that sense. She also caught the implied promise in the words: "First . . . the children" which suggested then the pets. Jesus had come to bring the gospel first to the children of Israel with whom the covenant had been made. Only then would it be brought to all others (see Acts 13:46). The woman acknowledged that as proper and right, but then also pressed her claim for the mercy she sensed in the words of Jesus. Our Lord rejoiced in the woman's answer of faith and assured her that her daughter had been healed. He had not compromised his assignment.

This account certainly comforted Mark's Gentile readers. They then knew that from the beginning Jesus had included them also and not only when he first said, "You will be my witnesses in Jerusalem, and in all Judea and Samaria, and to the ends of the earth" (Acts 1:8). This was also a lesson the disciples had to begin to learn. Though Christ was sent to

Israel first, he was not sent for Israel only. It was just a priority of time and, sad to say, it was not a lesson perceived by Israel, the majority of whom rejected the Savior (see Acts 13:46-52). The Gentiles were not excluded, but included —even as this woman and her daughter before their time. Nor were these the only Gentiles with whom the Lord dealt so graciously (see Mark 5:1f; 7:31f).

The Healing of a Deaf and Mute Man

³¹Then Jesus left the vicinity of Tyre and went through Sidon, down to the Sea of Galilee and into the region of the Decapolis. ³²There some people brought a man to him who was deaf and could hardly talk, and they begged him to place his hand on the man.

³³After he took him aside, away from the crowd, Jesus put his fingers into the man's ears. Then he spit and touched the man's tongue. ³⁴He looked up to heaven and with a deep sigh said to him, *"Ephphatha"* (which means, "Be opened!"). ³⁵At this, the man's ears were opened, his tongue was loosened and he began to speak plainly.

³⁶Jesus commanded them not to tell anyone. But the more he did so, the more they kept talking about it. ³⁷People were overwhelmed with amazement. "He has done everything well," they said. "He even makes the deaf hear and the mute speak."
(Matthew 15:29-31)

From Tyre Jesus and his disciples journeyed north to Sidon, then east and south toward the Sea of Galilee, and then to the Decapolis (the Ten Cities), the area east of the Jordan River and southeast of the Sea of Galilee. Decapolis was a region of Hellenistic, that is, Greek culture, and therefore predominantly Gentile. Our Lord performed many miracles in Decapolis and also preached the word there. He again showed that Gentiles were not excluded from the kingdom of God.

We do not know how long this journey from Tyre to Decapolis took. During this time when Jesus shuns the public eye, he devotes his time to instructing his disciples privately — a very important task, since they were to take the gospel out into all the world.

Jesus had been in Decapolis once before (see 5:20). That time the people had asked him to leave when they suffered the loss of a herd of pigs. But the demon-possessed man whom Jesus healed had gone throughout the area proclaiming Jesus' power and mercy. This witness, by just one man, brought a remarkable change. When Jesus returned, crowds gathered (see Matthew 15:30 and Mark 7:33) and brought their sick to Jesus. Mark related just one of the healings Jesus performed, undoubtedly the most striking one.

The case was pathetic, beyond the ability of any physician to heal or even to improve — a man who was deaf and mute. Friends of the man brought him to Jesus. Since the man who was deaf and mute could neither understand easily nor express himself readily, Jesus took him aside privately. Then using some exceptional sign language, the Lord made him understand what he was about to do for him. Jesus placed his fingers in his ears; he would give him hearing. Jesus spit and touched his tongue; he would give him the ability to speak clearly. By looking up to heaven and sighing deeply Jesus showed the man the cure he was bringing him was more than an ordinary man could perform. It came from God. Then Jesus spoke one word, and the man was immediately and completely cured.

As we read that Aramaic word, "*Ephphatha*," we again hear the very syllables Jesus spoke. In that way Mark brings our Lord very close to us, even as he does in 5:41, where he quotes the Aramaic words Jesus spoke in raising Jairus's daughter from death. The reaction of the crowd is our reaction too as we through these words of Mark stand in the presence of him who can be nothing less than the Son of God. For only God can do what he did.

Jesus commanded the people not to tell anyone because the Jewish people of his day had a totally false, political conception of the coming Messiah. Christ made it clear that he had not come into this predominantly Gentile territory to organize a political insurrection. He had come on earth to lay down his life as a payment for the sins of the world. He was determined to let nothing compromise the purpose for which he had come.

Today the command not to tell anyone no longer applies. In fact, this is one of the great miracles of our Lord which we are to proclaim so that others too may come face to face with the divine power and love of the Savior and turn to him for all blessings, both temporal and spiritual.

Jesus Feeds the Four Thousand

8 **During those days another large crowd gathered. Since they had nothing to eat, Jesus called his disciples to him and said, ²"I have compassion for these people; they have already been with me three days and have nothing to eat. ³If I send them home hungry, they will collapse on the way, because some of them have come a long distance."**

⁴His disciples answered, "But where in this remote place can anyone get enough bread to feed them?"

⁵"How many loaves do you have?" Jesus asked.

"Seven," they replied.

⁶He told the crowd to sit down on the ground. When he had taken the seven loaves and given thanks, he broke them and gave them to his disciples to set before the people, and they did so. ⁷They had a few small fish as well; he gave thanks for them also and told the disciples to distribute them. ⁸The people ate and were satisfied. Afterward the disciples picked up seven basketfuls of broken pieces that were left over. ⁹About four thousand men were

present. And having sent them away, **¹⁰he got into the boat with his disciples and went to the region of Dalmanutha.**
(Matthew 15:32-39)

This account of a second miraculous feeding by Christ of a multitude, this time 4,000, provides an opportunity to look at how modern Bible interpreters deal with Scripture. The majority of theologians in modern Christendom refuse to say with Christ, "The Scripture cannot be broken" (John 10:35) and, "Your word is truth" (John 17:17). They reject what Paul says in 2 Timothy 3:16: "All Scripture is God-breathed (inspired)." They reduce the authors of Scripture to writers having the same imperfections and being subject to the same errors as authors of writings not inspired by the Holy Spirit. They even state that many of the Scripture writers knowingly colored or manipulated what they wrote for their own purposes. For them this second feeding of a multitude seems to be made to order for their criticism. They insist that it is nothing but a duplicate of the feeding of the 5,000 (6:30-44). If this is true, then of course anything else Mark wrote or the other writers of the Bible recorded is subject to doubt.

Are the miracles identical? The differences between the two are so great that this is impossible. The locations are different — here the region of Decapolis, the other farther north. The 5,000 are with Jesus just one day, the 4,000 for three days. In the case of the 4,000 the disciples simply leave the matter up to Christ. In the other they beseech Jesus to send the people away. The number of loaves and fishes is different in both cases, to say nothing about the number of those who were fed. Even the Greek words for the baskets used to gather the fragments are different. At the feeding of the 5,000, small baskets such as the Israelites often used for carrying food and extra clothing are used. With the 4,000 the word used means a larger hamper. Finally, here our Lord leaves in a boat with his disciples, and the other time he goes up on a mountain to pray. The differences rule out any theory that these are two accounts of the same event.

Besides, Matthew also records both feedings. If both Evangelists had been in error, the church of that day would have said so, for other apostles were still alive as were many of the 4,000 and the 5,000. But these are not even our main witnesses. Later in this chapter (vv 17-21) Jesus speaks to his disciples about both feedings as separate events. It's almost as though our Lord knew in advance — he did! —how modern theologians and commentators would misinterpret the feedings of the 4,000 and the 5,000 to undermine faith and trust in the Scriptures. Jesus' words expose them for what they are — false teachers.

Now turn to the account itself and note Jesus' compassion. Not only was he concerned about the spiritual needs of the crowd (compare 6:34), but also about their physical needs. These 4,000 plus (see Matthew 15:38) had chosen to stay with Jesus three days. This exhausted any food supply they had brought along. They had stayed to hear him and to be healed of their diseases. Jesus could not ignore their physical needs, especially since many had come from far. As Jesus did in feeding the 5,000, so also here he began the meal with a blessing. It was a practice of our Lord which we ought not to forget today. Our groceries also are a gift of God. Again, there was plenty for all. And again, there was no waste; the leftovers were gathered, seven hampers full.

The feeding of the 4,000 took place in the Decapolis region predominantly Gentile in population and Greek in culture. This was also indicated in Matthew 15:31: "They praised the God of Israel." "They" were not Israelites. Again this would be of special comfort to the first readers of this

Gospel. And it also opens the door wide to most of those who belong to the church today — Gentiles.

Mark states that they took a boat to the region of Dalmanutha, whereas Matthew says "to the vicinity of Magadan." Both places have disappeared from the map. But the fact that "region" and "vicinity" are generalizations does not permit the critics to attack the texts as being contradictory. The region was a wilderness area that had many small villages.

The Pharisees Request a Sign from Heaven

11The Pharisees came and began to question Jesus. To test him, they asked him for a sign from heaven. 12He sighed deeply and said, "Why does this generation ask for a miraculous sign? I tell you the truth, no sign will be given to it." 13Then he left them, got back into the boat and crossed to the other side.
(Matthew 16:1-4)

Mark has abbreviated the account. Matthew recorded that the Pharisees did not approach Jesus alone, but were joined by the Sadducees. Hatred for Christ made for strange bed-fellows. They asked for a sign from heaven, a supernatural sign perhaps involving the sun, moon or stars. This showed they rejected the numerous signs Jesus had already given in demonstration of his divine power and love —the latest, the feeding of the 4,000. The Pharisees simply rejected all of Christ's miracles as so much magic or as done with the help of Satan (see 3:22). By describing their request as being done "to test him," Mark showed that their request was not sincere. They would not have believed in Jesus as the Son of God even if he had given them a sign such as Joshua had given, the sun's standing still (see Joshua 10:12-14). After all, wasn't Joshua just a human being, even though God had honored his command? Because of their unbelief Jesus re-

111

fused to give them the sign they requested, a refusal underscored by an oath. Their attitude filled Jesus with sorrow because it was representative of the entire generation.

Mark relates Christ told them, "No sign will be given." Matthew adds, "Except the sign of Jonah." This is not a contradiction, for the sign of Jonah, the resurrection of our Lord Jesus Christ, does not involve the heavens.

The sign the Pharisees were demanding was one they had no right to demand. Christ had not been sent to make a spectacular demonstration of his deity, but had been sent to fulfill the promises given in the Old Testament, namely, to lay down his life for the sins of the world, even for the sins of his enemies. But they would not believe. How sad!

The Yeast of the Pharisees and Herod

14The disciples had forgotten to bring bread, except for one loaf they had with them in the boat. 15"Be careful," Jesus warned them. "Watch out for the yeast of the Pharisees and that of Herod."

16They discussed this with one another and said, "It is because we have no bread."

17Aware of their discussion, Jesus asked them: "Why are you talking about having no bread? Do you still not see or understand? Are your hearts hardened? 18Do you have eyes but fail to see, and ears but fail to hear? And don't you remember? 19When I broke the five loaves for the five thousand, how many basketfuls of pieces did you pick up?"

"Twelve," they replied.

20"And when I broke the seven loaves for the four thousand, how many basketfuls of pieces did you pick up?"

They answered, "Seven."

21He said to them, "Do you still not understand?"
(Matthew 16:5-12)

As the disciples left the ship, they discovered that in their haste they had forgotten to bring along food. They had with them only one loaf, not enough to feed the group by any stretch of the imagination.

But Jesus, still thinking about the feeding of the 4,000 and his subsequent run-in with the Pharisees and the adherents of Herod whom Matthew in his account of the same incident calls the Sadducees, warned his disciples against the yeast of the Pharisees and of Herod. By this he meant the principles and teachings they championed. The Pharisees (7:1-23) added their own interpretations to God's law and insisted that keeping these traditions made them acceptable to God. In doing so they undermined the gospel message of the Old Testament centered in Christ even as the New Testament, and also undermined the moral law given by God himself. The followers and friends of Herod, the Sadducees, took a very rationalistic attitude toward life, rejected most of the Old Testament, and denied doctrines such as the resurrection of the body and the existence of angels. Jesus here warned his own disciples against permitting such destructive notions to find a place in their hearts. It is no wonder that Paul later writes twice to his readers: "A little yeast works through the whole batch of dough" (1 Corinthians 5:6; Galatians 5:9). Even a little false doctrine can rob a person of the Savior and of his saving gospel.

The disciples, their minds filled with the earthly concern of the moment, foolishly thought he was chiding them for having neglected to bring food along. That concern was indeed foolish, as Jesus promptly showed them and thus revealed to them that they did not have their hearts focused on spiritual matters as they should have. The lack of bread should not have bothered disciples who had collected twelve lunch baskets of bread when Christ fed the 5,000, and seven hampers of bread when he fed the 4,000. After all, wasn't he with them, and was food really to be the chief concern of their lives?

Matthew's account assures us that the disciples finally came to understand Christ, and Jesus' final question in Mark's record suggests the same. If the disciples needed to be reminded, we also need that reminder. Food for the body is not the main thing in life, and we must be extremely careful that we supply for our souls the food which causes us to grow in Christ. Instead of pointing to people called Pharisees and Sadducees and followers of Herod, our Lord today warns us against liberalism, legalism, millennialism, unitarianism, universalism and the hundred and one other false teachings. Any doctrine that robs us of Christ is spiritual poison. Watch out for that yeast!

The Healing of a Blind Man at Bethsaida

²²They came to Bethsaida, and some people brought a blind man and begged Jesus to touch him. ²³He took the blind man by the hand and led him outside the village. When he had spit on the man's eyes and put his hands on him, Jesus asked, "Do you see anything?"

²⁴He looked up and said, "I see people; they look like trees walking around."

²⁵Once more Jesus put his hands on the man's eyes. Then his eyes were opened, his sight was restored, and he saw everything clearly. ²⁶Jesus sent him home, saying, "Don't go into the village."

Only Mark records this miracle. Jesus and his disciples were still in semi-seclusion near Bethsaida on the northeastern end of the Sea of Galilee, not too far from where Jesus had fed the 5,000. It was here some people brought a blind man to Jesus for healing. It is clear they believed Jesus could do so, but nothing is stated about the blind man himself. That undoubtedly was the reason why Jesus dealt with him as he did. How considerate the Lord was as he took the blind man by the hand and led him outside Bethsaida, where they would not be disturbed. The man had something to learn, not only to receive, and so Jesus dealt with him in a way that opened his understanding.

First, Jesus let him know that he would indeed heal his blindness, as he put saliva from his own mouth on the man's eyes — something the man could feel. Then, Jesus laid his hands on him as the man's friends had requested. Next, Jesus asked him whether he could see, perhaps causing him to open his eyes and take a look. He saw large, blurred tree-like figures moving about. Since trees don't move, the blind man supposed he saw men. Evidently he had not been born blind, otherwise how would he have known what trees look like. The men whom he saw were the men who had brought him or the Lord's disciples. His heart was filled with hope. Finally, when Jesus then placed his hands on him for the second time, his sight was restored. He had 20/20 vision.

The unique feature of this miracle was its two stages. But who said that Jesus must always perform miracles in the same way? Here he adapted his method to the man's needs.

After healing him, Jesus sent him directly home. A crowded village would not have been the proper place for him to spend the next hours; the excitement in his family circle was more than enough. He needed time to meditate on what Christ had done for him. A question undoubtedly suggested itself to his heart: "Who is this Jesus, who gave me back my sight? Can he be just a man, and no more?"

Peter's Confession of Christ

27Jesus and his disciples went on to the villages around Caesarea Philippi. On the way he asked them, "Who do people say I am?"

28They replied, "Some say John the Baptist; others say Elijah; and still others, one of the prophets."

²⁹"But what about you?" he asked. "Who do you say I am?" Peter answered, "You are the Christ."
³⁰Jesus warned them not to tell anyone about him.
(Matthew 16:13-20; Luke 9:18-21)

During all the time spent in the area of Caesarea Philippi at the northern end of the Jordan River valley, Jesus continued to instruct his disciples. The time now came for a test. How well had they learned what he sought to impart to them?

As you review the miracles our Lord performed and the words he spoke as recorded by Mark — and we are now halfway through the Gospel — what are your answers to the questions Jesus put to the Twelve?

Jesus' first question was preliminary: "Who do people say I am?" The answers varied. Some said he was John the Baptist, others Elijah, and still others one of the prophets. All these answers involved a resurrection from the dead and thus were answers the Sadducees would not have given. They were answers given by such who were taking a serious look at Christ. For them he was more than just another teacher; he was clearly bringing a message from God himself. Yet all these answers made Jesus out to be a man, and no more. They were inadequate, as the first verse of Mark's Gospel informed us.

So Jesus proceeded to the next question, the vital one: "But what about you? Who do you say I am?" Since they had lived with Jesus on an intimate basis, they indeed knew he was a true man. He needed food; he needed rest. However they had also seen him perform miracles no man could do by his own powers. They had heard the demons and the demon-possessed speak of him as the Son of God. They had heard him claim the authority on earth to forgive sins. But over against that they had also seen how the people of his hometown and the theologically trained teachers of the law had rejected him. They remembered what they had asked themselves when he had stilled the violent storm on the Sea of Galilee: "Who is this? Even the wind and the waves obey him!" (4:41). Had they now come to a conviction as to who he was? They had, and Peter spoke for them all: "You are the Christ."

What did Peter mean? The Greek word "Christ" is the same as the Hebrew word "Messiah" and means "the Anointed One," one consecrated and appointed by God. Was the Messiah promised in the Old Testament just a man? He was indeed spoken of as prophet, priest and king. Yet Caiaphas put it correctly when he questioned Jesus at his trial: "Are you the Christ, the Son of the Blessed One?" (14:61). Yes, the Messiah, though truly human, was also God the Son, and his assignment as the Anointed One was clearly stated in Genesis 3:15, Isaiah 53 and Isaiah 9:6,7. He was and is the Savior.

However the people of Jesus' day and for centuries before had added a political connotation to the name Messiah. They expected his kingdom to be an earthly one, even as the millennialists do today. Therefore Jesus avoided using the name for himself before he accomplished his mission. Even the disciples had not rid themselves of these erroneous ideas, as we see in verse 33 of this chapter and in Acts 1:6. So although Jesus joyfully accepted Peter's answer as valid (see Matthew 16:17-19), he nevertheless warned the disciples not to tell anyone he was the Christ.

The answer of the Twelve, as given by Peter, is the very one Christ hoped for. It is also our answer. Jesus is the Son of God and the Son of Man, our Christ, our Savior and our Redeemer.

Teaching the Disciples

JESUS REVEALED AS THE CHRIST, THE SON OF GOD, IN HIS SUFFERING, DEATH AND RESURRECTON

Jesus' Final Days in Galilee
Jesus Predicts His Death

³¹He then began to teach them that the Son of Man must suffer many things and be rejected by the elders, chief priests and teachers of the law, and that he must be killed and after three days rise again. ³²He spoke plainly about this, and Peter took him aside and began to rebuke him.

³³But when Jesus turned and looked at his disciples, he rebuked Peter. "Get behind me, Satan!" he said. "You do not have in mind the things of God, but the things of men."

(Matthew 16:21-23; Luke 9:22)

This was the first time, as recorded by Mark, that Jesus explicitly predicted his coming passion. Before this he had only spoken about it in a veiled way (see 2:19,20). From here on, however, he spoke plainly and repeatedly about it (see 9:9-13,31,32; 10:32-34). He did so in order that his disciples might understand that his being the Christ, as Peter had confessed him in their name, did not make him an earthly king — a false hope that continued to linger in their hearts until his ascension. That's why Jesus did not as a rule speak of himself as Christ, but as the Son of Man.

Jesus began teaching the disciples by saying that "the Son of Man *must* suffer," etc. He said "must" because that was what the Old Testament taught (see Genesis 3:15; Psalm 118:22; Isaiah 50:6; Isaiah 53). By saying "must," Jesus informed his disciples that this was something that could not be avoided if all people were to be saved.

Now the Old Testament did not explicitly say who would cause Christ to suffer and die. It hinted at it by saying it would be the "builders" who would reject the "cornerstone." However Jesus identified the very men and showed he knew the future. His words were therefore true prophecy when he designated those who would reject and condemn him as "the elders, chief priests and teachers of the law." These were the men who constituted the seventy-one members of the Jewish high court, the Sanhedrin, which had two areas of responsibility, religious and political, in Judea. And when Jesus said the Son of Man must be killed, he also involved the Roman governor. The Sanhedrin at that time no longer possessed the authority to carry out the death sentence, but the procurator did. Thus Jesus clearly stated through whom his suffering and death would happen.

He also added a note of final victory. After three days he would rise again. But this the disciples constantly forgot, so shocked were they by the fact that he, their Lord and Master, would suffer and die. That's why the resurrection actually took them by surprise.

The words "after three days" at first glance seem not to be in accordance with the fact that "on" the third day Christ rose from the dead. However, this was the Hebrew way of speaking. "After three days" did not necessarily mean after three full days, but the passing of parts of three days. In this case they were the afternoon (Friday) Christ died, the day (Saturday) his body was in the grave, and the morning (Sunday) he rose again.

Perhaps the most shocking element in this account is Peter's taking Jesus aside to rebuke him, that is, to try to persuade him under no circumstance to suffer and die. It shows us that his and the other disciples' understanding of the name "Christ" was corrupted by false expectations. That's why Jesus in answering Peter directs the answer to all the disciples. They all need correction.

Jesus' answer at first glace seems overly harsh. It wasn't because Peter in speaking to Christ as he did was really, though unknowingly, championing the cause of Satan. This also was the same temptation Satan had set before Christ in the wilderness. It also agreed completely with what we usually want for ourselves — power and glory without any suffering. But it did not agree with God's plan of salvation. Thank God, Jesus answered as he did. He rejected Peter's wellmeant but ill-conceived rebuke. Without Christ's suffering, death and resurrection we would still be in our sins and lost forever.

Discipleship and Its Price

34Then he called the crowd to him along with his disciples and said: "If anyone would come after me, he must deny himself and take up his cross and follow me. 35For whoever wants to save his life will lose it, but whoever loses his life for me and for the gospel will save it. 36What good is it for a man to gain the whole world, yet forfeit his soul? 37Or what can a man give in exchange for his soul? 38If anyone is ashamed of me and my words in this adulterous and sinful generation, the Son of Man will be ashamed of him when he comes in his Father's glory with the holy angels."

9 And he said to them, "I tell you the truth, some who are standing here will not taste death before they see the kingdom of God come with power."

(Matthew 16:24-28; Luke 9:23-27)

Jesus addressed these words to a crowd as well as to his disciples. Their contents were a natural and proper sequence to the two foregoing events. Christ had asked his disciples whom they considered him to be. He immediately corrected their worldly expectations by telling them that as Christ he would have to suffer and die. Then he told the crowd and his disciples what it meant to follow this Son of Man who was to suffer and die.

Many in the crowds had been following Christ for entirely material reasons. Many were also defecting (see John 6:60-66), when it became clear that Jesus would not consent to become an earthly king (see John 6:14,15). By not luring and bribing them with false promises of worldly glory or free food, Jesus demonstrated his own dedication to the mission on which the Father had sent him. He faced his own destiny squarely, and he told the crowd and his disciples that if they followed him they would face the same destiny.

Following Christ means denying oneself, that is, refusing to make oneself the sole object in one's life, but making God and his will the center of one's life. That will always involve sacrifices, avoiding everything that might come between us and our Savior (see 7:20-23), even taking up a cross and being ready to suffer shame and death to remain faithful to him.

Mark's first readers had already experienced that in their lives and were to experience even more. Christians today also are not being spared. In many countries they are being persecuted because of their faith. In our own country atheistic propaganda is growing more powerful and, at times, even influences laws and courts. The cross and being loyal to Christ always go together (see 1 Peter 4:12-16).

Is the Christian life worthwhile? Christ tells us that whoever denies him and thus seeks to salvage a beautiful earthly existence will lose his life. That person will end up in damnation. Losing one's earthly life for Christ and the gospel means keeping eternal life. Most of us today are not asked to bring that great a sacrifice. By taking the Lord's promise of eternal life into consideration, we can easily answer our Lord's next two questions: "What good is it for a man to gain the whole world, yet forfeit his soul?" and "What can a man give in exchange for his soul?" Possessing the whole world (and who achieves that?) is not worth losing one's soul, but the sad fact is many will sacrifice their salvation for a great deal less.

Lest anyone think it isn't really that serious, Jesus finally points to judgment day and clearly states that when he comes as judge, he will reject all who in this life were ashamed of him. As we read these words, let's not shrug our shoulders, say we have plenty of time, or perhaps even hope for a second chance after death. The final chapter is written in this life. Faith is a gift; let's not throw it away. These words also add another dimension to what it means to be the Christ, the Son of God.

Lest the disciples and the crowd be tempted to turn away, saying, "Those are just so many words," Christ emphatically pointed to the evidence of his power which many standing there that day would live to see. Jesus did not refer to judgment day, for he himself as the Son of Man was not given to know the day or hour (see 13:32), but to the marvelous growth of the Christian church, which in the course of the next thirty plus years spread over much of the Mediterranean world (read the Book of Acts). Before Jerusalem was destroyed in A.D. 70, there were Christian congregations in Israel, Egypt, Asia Minor, Greece and Italy. Christ's kingdom was firmly established before the apostles died.

The church today also faces the cross, but the kingdom still comes with power, as the mission fields bring to our attention. The Lord Jesus also places a question before you: Will you be a follower of his? If so, there will be a cross to bear. But there will also be a crown of glory on the last day. Is it worth it, or will you betray the Lord as Judas did for thirty pieces of silver and as Demas did "because he loved this world" (2 Timothy 4:10)?

Are you puzzled that verse 1 of chapter 9 is discussed with the last section of chapter 8? The text of the original Hebrew and Greek manuscripts of the Bible was divided into neither chapters nor verses. These were rather recent developments done to facilitate reference. It is uncertain whether the present chapter divisions are to be credited to Cardinal Hugh of Saint Cher (about 1340) or preferably to Stephen Langton, archbishop of Canterbury, who died in 1228. Even before the invention of printing, this division into chapters had already passed from the Latin manuscripts to those of other languages.

The division into verses is even more recent. For the Old Testament it goes back to the oldest known Hebrew manuscripts and came into general use in the 15th century. The present verse division in the New Testament was introduced by Robert Stephens in his Greek-Latin Testament in 1551. Since these divisions were not made by the inspired writers, they are not necessarily valid and remain a matter of human judgment as in this instance.

The Transfiguration

2After six days Jesus took Peter, James and John with him and led them up a high mountain, where they were all alone. There he was transfigured before them. 3His clothes became dazzling white, whiter than anyone in the world could bleach them. 4And there appeared before them Elijah and Moses, who were talking with Jesus.

5Peter said to Jesus, "Rabbi, it is good for us to be here. Let us put up three shelters — one for you, one for Moses and one for Elijah." 6(He did not know what to say, they were so frightened.)

⁷Then a cloud appeared and enveloped them, and a voice came from the cloud: "This is my Son, whom I love. Listen to him!"

⁸Suddenly, when they looked around, they no longer saw anyone with them except Jesus.

⁹As they were coming down the mountain, Jesus gave them orders not to tell anyone what they had seen until the Son of Man had risen from the dead. ¹⁰They kept the matter to themselves, discussing what "rising from the dead" meant.

¹¹And they asked him, "Why do the teachers of the law say that Elijah must come first?"

¹²Jesus replied, "To be sure, Elijah does come first, and restores all things. Why then is it written that the Son of Man must suffer much and be rejected? ¹³But I tell you, Elijah has come, and they have done to him everything they wished, just as it is written about him."

(Matthew 17:1-13; Luke 9:28-36)

Six days passed. Christ spent them in instructing his disciples. Luke 9:28 has "about eight days after." Recall what was said about "after three days" in Mark 8:31. By calling attention to the lapse of time, as three Evangelists do, they show there is a close connection between what Jesus told his disciples concerning his passion and what is about to happen here. The transfiguration very likely took place in the region of Caesarea Philippi. However we cannot identify the specific mountain.

Jesus took Peter, James and John and went to the mountain top to be alone with them. The Savior spent time in prayer, but the disciples fell asleep (see Luke 9:29,32). These three had been his chosen witnesses when he had raised Jairus's daughter (5:37), and they would be with him in Gethsemane. In Jairus's home he had revealed himself as having the power of God over death. In the garden he would address God as his Father. The transfiguration would reveal his divine nature in a visible way and also support the truthfulness of all he had told them in predicting his passion, which they were not ready to accept.

What happened on the mountain was startling. The three awoke and saw Jesus. His clothes were an unearthly white, and his face shone like the sun (see Matthew 17:2). When Moses returned from the presence of God, "his face was radiant" (Exodus 34:35), but in his case that was simply a reflection of the glory of God. In Jesus' case the radiance came from within, a revelation of his divine nature. This supports what Peter previously had said, "You are the Christ" (8:29), "the Son of the living God" (Matthew 16:16).

But this wasn't all they were privileged to experience. With Jesus in glory there also appeared Moses and Elijah. The three disciples knew them without being introduced. (Does this tell us something about heaven?) The three listened in on a very instructive conversation, for "they spoke about his departure, which he was about to bring to fulfillment at Jerusalem" (Luke 9:31). Jesus had revealed this very thing to his disciples when he said, "The Son of Man must suffer many things and be rejected . . . and he must be killed and after three days rise again" (8:31).

Moses was the representative of the law. The law, or Torah, meant not only the commandments, but the entire good and gracious will of God, including the gospel (see Genesis 3:15 and Deuteronomy 18:15-19). Elijah was the great prophet who by the power of God succeeded in bringing many in Israel back to God at a time when God himself said, "I reserve seven thousand in Israel — all whose knees have not bowed down to Baal" (1 Kings 19:18). He had been taken to heaven without suffering death. The presence and the words of these two prophets assured the disciples that God's purpose was being fulfilled in Christ, in exactly the way Christ had told them.

Their presence also has an important message for us today. It shows Christianity is not a new religion, a breakaway from the Old Testament faith. Not at all! It is the continuation and fulfillment. Christianity began in the Garden of Eden and will reach its marvelous climax on Judgment Day. Those who reject Christ actually reject Moses and Elijah, even though they may use their words in their religious ceremonies. Moses and Elijah are on the side of Christ.

We can understand Peter's reaction as he said, "Let us put up three shelters" — like those for the Feast of Tabernacles — one for Jesus, one for Elijah, one for Moses. Undoubtedly it was to prolong the thrilling experience. But then the disciples would have failed to receive the greatest lesson of all.

Suddenly they were enveloped by a cloud — something they recognized from the Old Testament as the presence of God. And from the cloud the voice of the heavenly Father said, "This is my Son, whom I love. Listen to him!" Undoubtedly this also strengthened Jesus in his determination to be the Lamb of God who takes away the sins of the world. Yet the words were addressed specifically to the disciples. God assured them of three marvelous facts: 1) Jesus Christ is my Son; 2) I love him, that is, I fully approve of what he is doing; 3) You listen to him, that is, what he says is the truth. It didn't take long for these words to be uttered; it took much longer for their truth to sink in.

As suddenly as it began, the transfiguration came to an end. Only Jesus remained — the Son of God to whom they were to listen. As had happened before, Jesus told them not to tell anyone about what they had seen and heard. If they had proclaimed this truth before he had fulfilled his suffering, dying and rising again, it would have been misused and not believed.

127

But the disciples did have some personal questions. After having seen his glory, they were unable to reconcile that with his death and rising again. There were also other matters that puzzled them. They had heard the teachers of the law, on the basis of Malachi 3:1 and 4:5,6, teach that Elijah would appear before the coming of the Messiah. Was this appearance of Elijah at the transfiguration what Malachi had been talking about? It didn't seem so.

Jesus assured them what the teachers of the law were saying about Elijah was correct, and pointed to John the Baptist as the Elijah who was to come. When we study what John the Baptist did in his ministry as forerunner of Christ, we see that is exactly what had been foretold (compare Mark 1:2-8 with Malachi 4:5,6). The judgment was fulfilled in a preliminary way with the destruction of Jerusalem, and it will be fulfilled in its final form on the last day. But note that none of the prophecies say that this was to be an action performed by Elijah or by John the Baptist, but a judgment carried out by God himself and by our Lord Jesus Christ.

The three witnesses to the transfiguration kept this to themselves until after the resurrection. One of them, James, was the first to come into the presence of Jesus in the glory of heaven, when he was executed by Herod about A.D. 41. Peter wrote about the transfiguration in 2 Peter 1:16-18. John, while still here on earth, once again saw the Lord in his glory, as he wrote in Revelation 1:10-19. And Mark wrote what he had heard directly from Peter.

The Healing of a Boy with an Evil Spirit

[14]When they came to the other disciples, they saw a large crowd around them and the teachers of the law arguing with them. [15]As soon as all the people saw Jesus, they were overwhelmed with wonder and ran to greet him.

[16]"What are you arguing with them about?" he asked.

¹⁷A man in the crowd answered, "Teacher, I brought you my son, who is possessed by a spirit that has robbed him of speech. ¹⁸Whenever it seizes him, it throws him to the ground. He foams at the mouth, gnashes his teeth and becomes rigid. I asked your disciples to drive out the spirit, but they could not."
¹⁹"O unbelieving generation," Jesus replied, "how long shall I stay with you? How long shall I put up with you? Bring the boy to me."
²⁰So they brought him. When the spirit saw Jesus, it immediately threw the boy into a convulsion. He fell to the ground and rolled around, foaming at the mouth.
²¹Jesus asked the boy's father, "How long has he been like this?" "From childhood," he answered. ²²"It has often thrown him into fire or water to kill him. But if you can do anything, take pity on us and help us."
²³" 'If you can'?" said Jesus. "Everything is possible for him who believes."
²⁴Immediately the boy's father exclaimed, "I do believe; help me overcome my unbelief!"
²⁵When Jesus saw that a crowd was running to the scene, he rebuked the evil spirit. "You deaf and mute spirit," he said, "I command you, come out of him and never enter him again."
²⁶The spirit shrieked, convulsed him violently and came out. The boy looked so much like a corpse that many said, "He's dead."²⁷But Jesus took him by the hand and lifted him to his feet, and he stood up.
²⁸After Jesus had gone indoors, his disciples asked him privately, "Why couldn't we drive it out?"
²⁹He replied, "This kind can come out only by prayer."
(Matthew 17:14-21; Luke 9:37-43)

The symptoms described here are so similar to what we know as epilepsy that many commentators, who in their own hearts deny the possibility of demon possession and even reject the existence of Satan and his evil angels, say that this was actually a case of epilepsy. They claim that Mark, in writing as he did, reflected the mood and beliefs of his time which, according to them, falsely ascribed many illnesses to demon possession. However since what Mark wrote is "God-breathed" according to 2 Timothy 3:16, such commentators are really saying that God doesn't know what he's saying or that he accommodated himself to the beliefs of that day. We cannot accept either of these judgments, as was already pointed out in connection with Mark 1:21-28.

This was Mark's last account of the driving out of a demon by our Lord Jesus Christ. One element in all the healings with evil spirits was totally different from the miraculous healing of those who were sick. In each case of the healing of a demon-possessed person — with the exception in 7:24-30, where the girl herself was not personally present — there was always a confrontation between the demon and Jesus. See 1:23-26; 3:11,12; 5:7,8; and now 9:20,25,26. That sets these healings apart from such as that of Peter's mother-in-law (1:30,31) or of the paralytic (2:1-12), etc.

From the heights of the transfiguration Jesus and the three disciples descended to the realities of life with all its sin and sorrow. As they came to the nine disciples, Jesus found the teachers of the law arguing with them in the presence of a crowd. The nine were having real difficulty in defending themselves against the teachers of the law. Both sides recognized the disciples' inability to heal this demon-possessed lad as actually reflecting on Jesus himself. Jesus' return was opportune timing.

The question Jesus directed to the teachers of the law was answered by the father of the young lad. The picture he painted of his son's condition — an only child (see Luke 9:38) — was woeful. But the really sad part he had to report was that the disciples had been unable to heal the boy. That explains Jesus' next words. He was now well into the third year of instructing his disciples and thus wondered out loud when they would ever learn. How much longer would it take?

Jesus then asked to have the lad brought to him. This implied a promise to do something about his situation. The father answered, "If you can do anything, take pity on us and help us." The father's faith had nose-dived because the disciples had been unable to help him. But Jesus encouraged him, "Everything is possible for him who believes." The father in his anxiety cried out, even as we must so often in this life of ours, "I do believe; help me overcome my unbelief!" It was a confession Jesus honored. For this father Jesus both healed his son and strengthened his faith. Even though many said, "He's dead," when Jesus lifted him by his hand, the lad was healed completely.

But there were others also who needed help — the disciples. In private they asked Jesus, "Why couldn't we?" After all, Jesus had given them authority to do just that when he had sent them out on their preaching tour (6:7), and they had in fact driven out many demons (6:13). Why not now? "This kind," Jesus said, "can come out only by prayer." When the disciples' first attempts had proved futile, they should have realized they needed to seek the Lord in prayer. This power was not inherent in them as it was in Jesus, who could simply say, "I command you" (v 25). They had much to learn.

In verse 29, as well as in Matthew 17:21, the King James Version has: "This kind can come out only by prayer *and fasting.*" Some older Greek manuscripts, which the translators of the NIV used, do not contain these two words. Perhaps they were added by later copyists. The "fasting" suggests that the healing of demon-possessed persons or any others depends at least in part on the act of fasting. Not so! Besides, there was no time for fasting when the father brought his son to the disciples.

131

Christ's Second Prediction of His Passion

30They left that place and passed through Galilee. Jesus did not want anyone to know where they were, 31because he was teaching his disciples. He said to them, "The Son of Man is going to be betrayed into the hands of men. They will kill him, and after three days he will rise." 32But they did not understand what he meant and were afraid to ask him about it."

(Matthew 17:22,23; Luke 9:43-45)

This is the second time Mark records Jesus as speaking explicitly concerning his coming passion. Even this time the disciples do not fully understand. In fact, it seems they fear to face the full disclosure, because they may hear more than they want to hear.

We have no reason to criticize them. All the facts have been known for more than 1,900 years. But there are still those who refuse to admit that sin — our sin! — made Jesus' suffering and death necessary, and that his resurrection is our assurance that our sins are actually paid for.

Jesus' second announcement of his passion adds a new element. The NIV in all three Gospel accounts translates: "The Son of Man is going to be betrayed into the hands of men" (Matthew 17:22; Mark 9:31; Luke 9:44). The King James Version translates the same Greek word as "shall be betrayed" in Matthew 17, "is delivered" in Mark 9, and "shall be delivered" in Luke 9. "Is delivered" really adds nothing to what Christ had told the disciples in Mark 8:31. Therefore "is going to be betrayed" is preferable. It's a clear statement that someone near to Christ will give him over to those who will kill him. No wonder the disciples are afraid to ask any further questions. Rather, they push his coming passion out of their minds, and instead argue about who of them will be the greatest in the coming kingdom of heaven.

Who Is the Greatest?

³³**They came to Capernaum. When he was in the house, he asked them, "What were you arguing about on the road?" ³⁴But they kept quiet because on the way they had argued about who was the greatest.**

³⁵**Sitting down, Jesus called the Twelve and said, "If anyone wants to be first, he must be the very last, and the servant of all."**

³⁶**He took a little child and had him stand among them. Taking him in his arms, he said to them, ³⁷"Whoever welcomes one of these little children in my name welcomes me; and whoever welcomes me does not welcome me but the one who sent me."**
(Matthew 18:1-6; Luke 9:46-48)

Christ's last stop in Capernaum is a busy one and is spent for the most part in instructing his disciples. Mark devotes the rest of this chapter to it, and Matthew all of chapter 18. Luke's account is by far the shortest. When Matthew tells us that the disciples came to Jesus with their question about who is the greatest in the kingdom of heaven, the very way he expresses it shows that something had preceded. Mark supplies that. Consequently, the different ways in which they present the development of the situation are not contradictory.

On the way to Capernaum Jesus noticed the disciples had been arguing among themselves. Because he knew they were coming up with wrong answers, he wanted them to put the question to him. When he approached them, they at first remained silent and felt guilty. But urged by the Lord, they put the question to him as reported in Matthew 18.

Why were they concerned about the matter of greatness? Not only was it very human, but perhaps Jesus' own actions had suggested it. For the second time he had taken three of them aside as special witnesses, first when he had healed Jairus's daughter and now on the mountain. The latter must

133

have intrigued the nine even more, since the three did not report what had happened there. And then there had been Jesus' own word to Simon, calling him Peter, a rock (see Matthew 16:17,18). All this was puzzling to men who as yet did not know the whole story as we do. At the same time it also revealed their sinful hearts, and Jesus was concerned about that.

Jesus gave them an answer entirely different from what they expected. In the kingdom of heaven greatness is not a matter of titles and authority. To be first means to be the last, to be the servant. No service is too lowly, not even meeting the needs of a child. Service means sacrificing your time, your talents, yourself for the sake of others, even when they do not realize or appreciate it. Yes, even helping a child in Jesus' name spiritually, physically or emotionally is great in the kingdom of God. When you do so in Jesus' name, that is, because you love Jesus, then you not only welcome Jesus into your heart and life, but also the Father who sent him. What could be greater? But it's the complete opposite of how the world looks at it. It was a lesson Jesus felt compelled to give his disciples again and again (see Mark 10:43,44; Matthew 23:8-12; Luke 22:24-27).

That Jesus used a child in illustrating his answer brings a needed lesson to our own age, an age with so many unwanted children and with a murderous mania for aborting children. It is only those who are members of the kingdom of heaven by faith in Christ Jesus who have the right answer and the right motivation. What greater reason can we have for sharing the gospel?

Whoever Is Not Against Us Is for Us

38"Teacher," said John, "we saw a man driving out demons in your name and we told him to stop, because he was not one of us."

³⁹"Do not stop him," Jesus said. "No one who does a miracle in my name can in the next moment say anything bad about me, ⁴⁰for whoever is not against us is for us. ⁴¹I tell you the truth, anyone who gives you a cup of water in my name because you belong to Christ will certainly not lose his reward."

⁴²"And if anyone causes one of these little ones who believe in me to sin, it would be better for him to be thrown into the sea with a large millstone tied around his neck."

(Luke 9:49,50)

When John heard the words about welcoming Christ and the one who sent him, a recent incident came to mind. The disciples had come upon a man who was driving out demons in Christ's name, but was not a member of Christ's band of disciples and certainly not one of the Twelve. They had ordered him to stop. Had they acted correctly? Wasn't the driving out of demons part of the authority Jesus had given to them? John's words showed both a concern for Jesus and also a concern for their rights as disciples. The first was proper, the other not.

Jesus promptly told them that they were wrong. That the man drove out demons in Jesus' name proved he was a believer, unless of course there would have been specific evidence to the contrary. Such, Jesus told the Twelve, would be rewarded by the Lord even if their deed was no greater than giving a cup of water in Jesus' name to those who were his.

This certainly means that we will never seek to prevent others from preaching and proclaiming Christ even if they are not part of our specific group. We must leave the final judgment to Christ himself. On our part we must rather be watchful lest by word or example we lead anyone astray, and Christ here even includes the little ones who believe in him. We must always ask ourselves: Does my life and do my deeds and words lead others to Christ or lead them into sin? If the latter, Christ here issues a serious warning to us. It will be better that before we ever lead anyone into sin we will forfeit our own lives by having a millstone — a large one, turned by a donkey or an ox — tied to our neck and then being cast into the sea. To sin is something dreadful, but to lead someone else into sin is definitely worse.

The Goal Worth Any Sacrifice

43"If your hand causes you to sin, cut it off. It is better for you to enter life maimed than with two hands to go into hell, where the fire never goes out. 45And if your foot causes you to sin, cut it off. It is better for you to enter life crippled than to have two feet and be thrown into hell. 47And if your eye causes you to sin, pluck it out. It is better for you to enter the kingdom of God with one eye than to have two eyes and be thrown into hell, 48where

" 'their worm does not die,
and the fire is not quenched.'
49Everyone will be salted with fire.

50"Salt is good, but if it loses its saltiness, how can you make it salty again? Have salt in yourselves, and be at peace with each other."

Our Lord uses graphic expressions to teach his disciples and us how important it is to fight sin. Sin leads to hell. Jesus uses the pictures of Isaiah 66:24 to describe hell. It's the place of eternal torment.

To "go into hell" means what will happen when we choose that which is evil. To "be thrown into hell" means to be condemned to hell; God pronounces the judgment. That is what all face who sell out to sin.

What price are we willing to pay to avoid hell? Jesus says we should be ready to cut off our hand, cut off our foot, pluck out our eye. Are these words to be taken literally?

Note that Christ says, "If your hand . . . if your foot . . . if your eye *causes* you to sin." Is it really the hand, the foot or the eye that do so? If so, what about the remaining foot, the other hand, the other eye? Jesus gives his disciples the key to understanding these words (7:17-23). It is a person's heart that is the source of sin, though the hand, the foot or the eye may be used to commit the sin. Jesus uses pictorial words, lest we take sin lightly.

So what then if, as a result of avoiding sin, we don't get everything out of life our evil heart desires and we enter life crippled? Remember, we are entering life — eternal life, the kingdom of God. That's worth any and every sacrifice. In heaven there are no cripples (see Philippians 3:21).

Jesus also points out how sin is overcome. He uses another figure of speech, salt used to make food palatable and to preserve it. Sometimes this salt will burn like fire. What can this salt be? It is God's word whose law burns and whose gospel heals. Christ also warns that this salt is to be used as God has given it. If it is desalted as many modern theologians attempt, it will not do what God wants it to do. Then the case is hopeless. Take God's word into your heart as it is, and you will have salt in yourself. By means of it you will also be able to be at peace with one another — a reference to the argument the disciples had about who was the greatest.

What about being at peace with ourselves? Although we fight against sin, we can never overcome it completely. Is our case hopeless? No, Christ had already assured his disciples that he can and does forgive sins (2:5-10). That is why he came, and that is why he was now going to Jerusalem to suffer and die and rise again. But, as these words of Jesus show, the fact that we have forgiveness in him dare never move us to take sin lightly.

Jesus on the Way to Jerusalem
Divorce

10 Jesus then left that place and went into the region of Judea and across the Jordan. Again crowds of people came to him, and as was his custom, he taught them.

²Some Pharisees came and tested him by asking, "Is it lawful for a man to divorce his wife?"

³"What did Moses command you?" he replied.

⁴They replied, "Moses permitted a man to write a certificate of divorce and send her away."

⁵"It was because your hearts were hard that Moses wrote you this law," Jesus replied. ⁶"But at the beginning of creation God 'made them male and female.' ⁷For this reason a man will leave his father and mother and be united to his wife, ⁸and the two will become one flesh.' So they are no longer two, but one. ⁹Therefore what God has joined together, let man not separate."

¹⁰When they were in the house again, the disciples asked Jesus about this. ¹¹He answered, "Anyone who divorces his wife and marries another woman commits adultery against her. ¹²And if she divorces her husband and marries another man, she commits adultery."

(Matthew 19:1-12; John 10:40)

Jesus then left Galilee, went through Samaria, entered Judea and crossed the Jordan River into Perea. The time for longer periods of seclusion with his disciples was past, and the time for his passion was drawing near. During these months he again spent time in teaching the crowds that gathered and in healing many of their number. He did not cease the instructing of his disciples, but used every possible opportunity to do so. Here it was on a matter that was an acute issue in his day and is also in ours, the matter of divorce.

Matthew's account reads somewhat differently than Mark's, but that is easily accounted for. Note that there were a number of Pharisees who came to Jesus. Undoubtedly more than one put hostile questions to Christ.

The question of the Pharisees was not a sincere one. They were trying to trap Jesus into saying something they could use to discredit him. The divorce question was made to order, since they themselves were not agreed on the proper interpretation of Moses' words (see Deuteronomy 24:1). Those who followed Rabbi Shammai said the only reason for divorce was moral indecency; those who followed Hillel said anything in a wife that did not please the husband was grounds for divorce. They expected Jesus to side with one or the other, and they would then have the opportunity to criticize him publicly.

Jesus met their challenge. First, he told them that Moses' regulation, which they had quoted, was simply a concession to their hardness of heart. It was an attempt to keep reasonable order in society and not at all a statement whereby God approved of divorce. Next, Jesus referred back to creation and called their attention to the principles God established for marriage. Then he gave them his own judgment, based on those principles: "So they are no longer two, but one. Therefore what God has joined together, let man not separate."

Only so is God's original intent carried out. Marriage thus is not a human arrangement. It is God who joins husband and wife together. The Greek word actually means "yoked together as a team." God wants marriage to be "so long as you both shall live" or "till death us do part." Marriage is not just a temporary convenience, but a lifelong commitment.

In his words to the disciples Jesus repeated what he had already said to the Pharisees (see Matthew 19:8,9), but added a new element foreign to the Jews and Pharisees of that day, something even the disciples had not heard until then. Christ said that a man who divorces his wife and marries another woman commits adultery against his wife. Then he said the same about a woman who divorces her husband and marries another man. Thus he placed men and women in this matter in the same category — adulterers. In those days men who divorced their wives simply did not think they were doing anything wrong or displeasing to God, and women likewise. Human nature has not changed. Divorce is a problem the church of today must face.

The Holy Spirit used Mark's account of this conversation with the Pharisees and the disciples to emphasize what God's plan for marriage was from the very beginning. He had Mark say nothing here about circumstances in which divorce may be permissible. That he did in Matthew 5:32; 19:9 and 1 Corinthians 7:10-15.

The Little Children and Jesus

13People were bringing little children to Jesus to have him touch them, but the disciples rebuked them. 14When Jesus saw this, he was indignant. He said to them, "Let the little children come to me, and do not hinder them, for the kingdom of God belongs to such as these. 15I tell you the truth, anyone who will not receive the kingdom of God like a little child will never enter it." 16And he took the children in his arms, put his hands on them and blessed them.

(Matthew 19:13-15; Luke 18:15-17)

This is one of the most delightful, most comforting, and at the same time saddest stories in the synoptic Gospels. We can, of course, try to excuse the disciples by saying that they sought to protect Jesus from needless interruptions and thus save his time for more important things. But that's exactly what is very sad about their action.

By preventing people from bringing their children to Jesus, the disciples revealed that they considered children too immature to profit from the Lord's attention and were not yet in need of the Savior. But Jesus took the side of the people who brought their children to him. In most cases they undoubtedly were the parents.

Only once before did Mark tell us that Jesus became indignant or angry. That time (3:5) it was against the Pharisees. Here it was against his own disciples and rightly so. They should have known by this time that Jesus' blessings are there for all regardless of age. After all, he had brought Jairus's twelve-year-old daughter back to life. He had cured the Syrophoenician woman's daughter from demon possession. And just a few days before in Capernaum he had set a child in their midst to teach them what it meant to be great. How could they have been so imperceptive, so dull?

Jesus' words clearly teach that children, even "babies" —Luke 18:15 in recounting this incident uses that word —are to be brought into his kingdom. How sad then that some still today deny baptism to little children, as though baptism were not a gift of God but rather an act of obedience on the person's part! That in no way agrees with what Jesus told his disciples, "Let the little children come to me, for the kingdom of God belongs to such as these." These words of Jesus, and others such as those of Paul in Ephesians 6:4, are also the basis for our vacation Bible schools, Sunday schools and Christian day schools.

That Jesus is not speaking only about children, or only about the children that were present that particular day, becomes clear from his words: "The kingdom of God belongs to such as these," and his following words: "Anyone who will not receive the kingdom of God like a little child will never enter it." He is talking not only about children, but about people of all ages. The only way we can enter the kingdom is "like a little child," that is, by simple faith and trust in what Christ has done for us. Membership in the kingdom is not something we earn or merit by our own good deeds or exemplary life. These are fruits of being in the kingdom. We can merit the kingdom no more than a little child or a baby can. It is a gift of God's grace.

The Rich Young Man

¹⁷As Jesus started on his way, a man ran up to him and fell on his knees before him. "Good teacher," he asked, "what must I do to inherit eternal life?"

¹⁸"Why do you call me good?" Jesus answered. "No one is good — except God alone. ¹⁹You know the commandments: 'Do not murder, do not commit adultery, do not steal, do not give false testimony, do not defraud, honor your father and mother.' "

²⁰"Teacher," he declared, "all these I have kept since I was a boy."

²¹Jesus looked at him and loved him. "One thing you lack," he said. "Go, sell everything you have and give to the poor, and you will have treasure in heaven. Then come, follow me."

²²At this the man's face fell. He went away sad, because he had great wealth.

²³Jesus looked around and said to his disciples, "How hard it is for the rich to enter the kingdom of God!"

²⁴The disciples were amazed at his words. But Jesus said again, "Children, how hard it is to enter the kingdom of God! ²⁵It is easier for a camel to go through the eye of a needle than for a rich man to enter the kingdom of God."

²⁶The disciples were even more amazed, and said to each other, "Who then can be saved?"

²⁷Jesus looked at them and said, "With man this is impossible, but not with God; all things are possible with God."

²⁸Peter said to him, "We have left everything to follow you!"

²⁹"I tell you the truth," Jesus replied, "no one who has left home or brothers or sisters or mother or father or children or fields for me and the gospel ³⁰will fail to receive a hundred times as much in this present age (homes, brothers, sisters, mothers, children and

fields — and with them, persecutions) and in the age to come, eternal life. ³¹But many who are first will be last, and the last first." *(Matthew 19:16-30; Luke 18:18-30)*

Jesus continued on his way to Jerusalem, where he would pay the price for mankind's salvation. It was then that a young man (see Matthew 19:20,22) cast himself on his knees before Jesus with a question Jesus indeed had the answer to. Though he was a ruler (see Luke 18:18), probably in a synagogue, this young man did not know the way to eternal life. He thought eternal life was to be gained by deeds a person would perform, but he was uncertain as to just what these deeds were. He came to Jesus because he thought Jesus had the answer. Only for him Jesus, though "good," was no more than a "teacher."

It was this misunderstanding Jesus sought to correct first. "Don't you know that only God is 'good,' only God is perfect, and only God can therefore provide salvation? Why then do you call me 'good'?" With this Jesus did not say that he was not God, but rather sought to have the young man reflect on why he was calling Jesus "good" and what implications that might have. It was to make him think. There was more involved than just coming to Jesus with a question and seeking an answer.

The man had asked, "What must I do?" As ruler in a synagogue he had given the answer to many others. Jesus now gave him the same one — God's commandments. Jesus referred only to those that had to do with the young man's dealing with his fellowmen because these would have been the ones he would have felt the surest about. And he did. "All these I have kept since I was a boy." Why then his question? Although he had done everything, he felt dissatisfied. Today many people would reply that those commandments no longer apply and that eternal life is just imagination. They are worse off than this young ruler. He had lived an exemplary life. But. . . .

Jesus' heart went out to him, and so Jesus zeroed in on his one great fault. Jesus told him to sell all he had and give to the poor. Thus he would rid himself of the wealth that he loved more than God and that was keeping him out of the kingdom of God. But not only that. After having rid himself of his idol, he was to come and follow Jesus.

The price was too high for the rich young man. He forgot to look at the prize — Jesus Christ, treasure in heaven, the kingdom of God. Did he ever return? We don't know.

Jesus then used this occasion to teach his disciples a needed lesson. "How hard it is (for those who trust in riches) to enter the kingdom of God!" They were shocked. Then Jesus added: "It is easier for a camel to go through the eye of a needle than for a rich man to enter the kingdom of God." Man simply cannot save himself, neither the rich young ruler nor the disciples nor anyone else. Work-righteousness does not appease God.

Is our case then hopeless? No, for Jesus says, "With man this is impossible, but not with God; all things are possible with God." God can even move an idolatrous rich man to set aside his riches and to rest his heart on God. That is the power of the gospel.

It was Peter again who spoke up, "We disciples have done exactly what you told the ruler to do. What about us?" He too had not fully grasped Jesus' words. So Jesus pointed to the evidences of the grace of God they were already experiencing and would continue to experience in eternity. There was no way the gift of eternal life could be looked upon as a recompense for their deeds. It was pure grace.

Jesus' words also comfort us in our life here on earth. Because we belong to Christ, flesh and blood relatives may spurn and ridicule us, and we may also suffer more serious persecutions. But Jesus assures us that we will have all we need in the family of our Lord Jesus Christ. His love dwelling in the hearts of believers will come to meet us. Those are bonds of love more precious than all earthly bonds of blood. They last into eternity.

But for Peter, for all the disciples, and for all of us there were final words of caution: "But many who are first will be last, and the last first." There were men like Judas, one of the Twelve, or Caiaphas and Annas, high priests of God's people. They thought of themselves as "first." They did not end that way. Judas's idol was thirty pieces of silver. The idols of Annas and Caiaphas were their positions. All ended up outside the kingdom. But many a simple believer, ignored and despised by the great of this world, but accepted by God, ends up "first."

Here the Lord is speaking about riches and how riches make adherence to the Savior so difficult. But not all the rich begin or end like this rich young ruler. Remember Abraham, David, Zacchaeus, Cornelius, Lydia and many others. The difference? By God's grace they did not serve their riches, but put their riches and themselves into the service of Christ and the gospel. There are many such Christians today. Likewise there are also many other barriers to salvation beside riches.

Jesus' Third Prediction of His Passion

[32]They were on their way up to Jerusalem, with Jesus leading the way, and the disciples were astonished, while those who followed were afraid. Again he took the Twelve aside and told them what was going to happen to him. [33]"We are going up to Jerusalem," he said, "and the Son of Man will be betrayed to the chief priests and teachers of the law. They will condemn him to death and will hand him over to the Gentiles, [34]who will mock him and spit on him, flog him and kill him. Three days later he will rise."
(Matthew 20:17-19; Luke 18:31-34)

145

Jesus' previous prophecies concerning his passion (8:31 and 9:31) and his reference to it on the way down the mountain from his transfiguration (9:9-12) filled the hearts of the Twelve with amazement when they now saw Jesus lead the way to Jerusalem. Did he really intend to carry out what he had said? And the others who followed Jesus were also filled with dread. They sensed that something momentous, mysterious and tragic was about to happen.

It was then that Jesus for the third time took the Twelve aside and again foretold his passion. This time his prediction was even more detailed. His passion would take place in Jerusalem. He would be betrayed. The Sanhedrin would put him on trial and condemn him. He would be turned over to the Gentiles, that is, to the Roman governor. At the hands of the Roman soldiers he would suffer many indignities and would then be crucified, the manner of execution the Romans meted out to all who were not Romans. But there would be victory at the end; he would rise from the grave to life again.

Even this time, as Luke reports, the disciples simply could not comprehend. But would you and I have understood all this before the fact, especially if our religious teachers had spoken of the Messiah as setting up an earthly kingdom?

The Ambitious Request of James and John

35Then James and John, the sons of Zebedee, came to him. "Teacher," they said, "we want you to do for us whatever we ask."
36"What do you want me to do for you?" he asked.
37They replied, "Let one of us sit at your right and the other at your left in your glory."
38"You don't know what you are asking," Jesus said. "Can you drink the cup I drink or be baptized with the baptism I am baptized with?"
39"We can," they answered.

Jesus said to them, "You will drink the cup I drink and be baptized with the baptism I am baptized with, ⁴⁰but to sit at my right or left is not for me to grant. These places belong to those for whom they have been prepared."

⁴¹When the ten heard this, they became indignant with James and John. ⁴²Jesus called them together and said, "You know that those who are regarded as rulers of the Gentiles lord it over them, and their high officials exercise authority over them. ⁴³Not so with you. Instead, whoever wants to become great among you must be your servant, ⁴⁴and whoever wants to be first must be slave of all. ⁴⁵For even the Son of Man did not come to be served, but to serve, and to give his life as a ransom for many."

(Matthew 20:20-28)

Although our Lord had just described his coming passion in greater detail than before, his disciples still did not understand. They believed him to be the Messiah but had ears only for the glory connected with being the Messiah, not for the suffering.

It was surprising that James and John brought this request to Jesus. As part of the inner circle they should have known better. But the human heart is by nature sinful. According to Matthew it was their ambitious mother who actually brought the request to Jesus. Mark put the words into the mouths of James and John and showed that they went along with her in their ambition.

More shocking was their preliminary request with which they sought to bind Jesus without his knowing what they were going to ask. Their request showed they believed Jesus could give them anything they might ask. That they first asked Jesus to assure them he would hints that they suspected Jesus might not approve. How right they were!

As to the request itself, how could such thoughts have come to them? Perhaps they were prompted by the promise Jesus had made his disciples in connection with the case of the rich young man. Peter had said, "We have left everything to follow you." Mark did not record Jesus' entire answer. Jesus also said to them, "I tell you the truth, at the renewal of all things, when the Son of Man sits on his glorious throne, you who have followed me will also sit on twelve thrones, judging the twelve tribes of Israel" (Matthew 19:28). James and John must have latched on to that promise and now came to request the most prominent and honorable seats, one on Jesus' right and the other on his left.

Jesus' answer was blunt. He told them right out that they did not know what they were asking. They did not understand that the way to the throne is one of suffering and death, his suffering and death that he had just spoken about. This suffering and death only one person could endure. Jesus would lay down his life for the sins of the world. He then asked them, "Can you drink that cup and be baptized with that baptism?" They did not understand. Rashly they replied, "We can." Jesus told them that they would indeed share in that suffering, but as far as the places on his right and left were concerned, the Father had already made those choices.

The ten were no better than James and John, but only sorry they hadn't thought of asking first. Lest this matter become a cause of strife among the Twelve, Jesus then instructed them on the enormous difference between the kingdoms of this world and the kingdom of heaven. Jesus presented himself as the outstanding example. The Son of Man came not to be served, but to serve.

The great on earth exercise authority; the great in God's kingdom are servants to one another. That is their greatness. Read the Gospels; the evidence is overwhelming.

At the very close of the conversation Jesus added a statement that is one of the most comforting we have from his lips. It reveals the goal of his coming passion. "The Son of

Man . . . [came] to give his life as a ransom for many." His death, even though outwardly it seemed to have been inflicted on him, was at the same time a voluntary sacrifice on his part whereby he paid for the sins of all.

But didn't Jesus say "many"? And doesn't that leave some out? The rest of the Scriptures show us that that would be a misunderstanding of his gracious words. Those for whom he died are "many" in contrast to the one Son of Man.

Blind Bartimaeus Receives His Sight

⁴⁶Then they came to Jericho. As Jesus and his disciples, together with a large crowd, were leaving the city, a blind man, Bartimaeus (that is, the Son of Timaeus), was sitting by the roadside begging. ⁴⁷When he heard that it was Jesus of Nazareth, he began to shout, "Jesus, Son of David, have mercy on me!"
⁴⁸Many rebuked him and told him to be quiet, but he shouted all the more, "Son of David, have mercy on me!"
⁴⁹Jesus stopped and said, "Call him."
So they called to the blind man, "Cheer up! On your feet! He's calling you." ⁵⁰Throwing his cloak aside, he jumped to his feet and came to Jesus.
⁵¹"What do you want me to do for you?" Jesus asked him.
The blind man said, "Rabbi, I want to see."
⁵²"Go," said Jesus, "your faith has healed you." Immediately he received his sight and followed Jesus along the road.
(Matthew 20:29-34; Luke 18:35-43)

The accounts of this healing in Matthew, Mark and Luke have what seem like insurmountable differences. Some commentators and theologians use these to question the inspiration of the Bible. Is there a solution? R.C.H. Lenski in his *Interpretation of St. Mark's and St. Luke's Gospels* (p 295) gives a solution that satisfies both us and the Scriptures. "At first glance a decided discrepancy seems to exist between Mark (Matthew): 'he was going out from Jericho,' and Luke: 'in his drawing near to Jericho.' One says, these blind men were healed when Jesus left Jericho, the other, when Jesus entered Jericho. To remove the supposed contradiction strange efforts are used, even to postulating three different healings. Yet the matter is simple. Jesus passed through Jericho (see Luke 19:1) and, though it was late in the day, no one asked him in. On the other side of the town Zacchaeus awaited Jesus, who called him down from the tree, and who retraced his steps, went back into Jericho, and spent the night at the publican's home. It was on this return that the blind men were healed. Luke separates the two events, because he wants to tell the story of Zacchaeus all in one piece, without inserting into it the healing of the blind men. Mark and Matthew omit the story of Zacchaeus. Thus all three evangelists are correct. The apparent contradiction fades away the moment we have all the facts." The accounts of Mark and Luke with one blind man do not imply he was the only one. Mark mentioned only Bartimaeus perhaps because he knew his name. Matthew was present in person at Jericho and himself saw the two blind beggars.

The only difference between this healing at Jericho and those that had preceded it — not including the cases of demon possession — was that Bartimaeus addressed Jesus as "Son of David." This is the only place in Mark where this title is used for Jesus. This title was recognized by those who knew their Old Testament as being messianic (see Isaiah 11:1; Jeremiah 23:5,6; Ezekiel 34:23,24). Jesus did not stop the man from using this title. The time had come for Israel to face the fact that Jesus of Nazareth was indeed the Messiah. And since Christ was now only fifteen miles northeast of Jerusalem, the stronghold of his opponents and the headquarters of the Roman governor, there was no longer any danger of an uprising to proclaim him king, as there had been when he fed the 5,000.

Jesus commended the blind man's faith. Nor was his faith a shallow, temporary emotion. He followed Jesus along the road. That road led to Jerusalem, to the cross and to the open tomb. The very fact that his name was still known when Mark wrote this Gospel suggests that he had perhaps become a well-known member of the Jerusalem congregation. Bartimaeus's persistence and his faith are a model for our own prayer life.

Jesus' Ministry in Jerusalem
The Triumphal Entry

11 As they approached Jerusalem and came to Bethphage and Bethany at the Mount of Olives, Jesus sent two of his disciples, 2saying to them, "Go to the village ahead of you, and just as you enter it, you will find a colt tied there, which no one has ever ridden. Untie it and bring it here. 3If anyone asks you, 'Why are you doing this?' tell him, 'The Lord needs it and will send it back here shortly.' "

4They went and found a colt outside in the street, tied at a doorway. As they untied it, 5some people standing there asked, "What are you doing, untying that colt?" 6They answered as Jesus had told them to, and the people let them go. 7When they brought the colt to Jesus and threw their cloaks over it, he sat on it. 8Many people spread their cloaks on the road, while others spread branches they had cut in the fields. 9Those who went ahead and those who followed shouted,

"Hosanna!"

"Blessed is he who comes in the name of the Lord!"

10"Blessed is the coming kingdom of our father David!"

"Hosanna in the highest!"

11Jesus entered Jerusalem and went to the temple. He looked around at everything, but since it was already late, he went out to Bethany with the Twelve.

(Matthew 21:1-11; Luke 19:28-44; John 12:12-16)

151

We know this day as Palm Sunday, the beginning of Holy Week. This was not the first time Jesus had come to Jerusalem since he began his ministry. The Gospel of John mentions three other times Jesus had visited Jerusalem (John 2:13; 5:1; 7:10). But this was the last time, and Jesus knew what he faced. Three times he had explicitly told his disciples that he would suffer and die there and on the third day rise again (8:31,32; 9:31; 10:32-34). So he went, ready to carry out the Father's will and to redeem mankind by his suffering and death. The disciples had confessed him as Christ, although they did not fully understand what that meant. In Jericho Bartimaeus had addressed him as the Son of David. Others had called him the Son of God. He came into Jerusalem on that first Palm Sunday to make a statement to the effect that he was all of those, but not in the sense the disciples and the crowds understood it. His statement concerning himself on Palm Sunday was understood properly by the disciples only after his ascension (see John 12:16) and by many of the people and even large numbers of priests after Pentecost (see Acts 6:7). For us the events of Palm Sunday support our faith in him as our Savior, Redeemer and King.

Having come to the Mount of Olives in the vicinity of Bethany and Bethphage, Jesus commanded two disciples to go into the nearby village and get a colt they would find there. If anyone were to ask them why they were untying the colt, they were to say that the Lord needed it and would return it shortly. Everything happened just as Jesus said. Certainly that strengthened their faith in him, for it was evidence of his supernatural knowledge. In fact, the very words he told them to speak declared who he was, declared his deity: "The *Lord* needs it." That the owners of the colt (see Luke 19:33) permitted the disciples to take the colt and its mother (see Matthew 21:7) indicated they too knew Jesus and trusted him. Undoubtedly they knew about the many miracles he had performed, particularly the last one — the raising of Lazarus. They were not about to doubt that he actually needed the colt and that he would send it back shortly. Jesus' command to bring a "colt, which no one has ever ridden," was a significant part of the statement Jesus made that day. It suggested according to Scripture (read Numbers 19:2; Deuteronomy 21:3; and 1 Samuel 6:7) that the colt as yet unused was to be used for a sacred purpose. What could be more sacred than to carry the Son of God into Jerusalem to begin his passion? But it had an even greater purpose. It reminded all who saw him ride into Jerusalem of the prophecy of Zechariah 9:9: "Rejoice greatly, O Daughter of Zion! Shout, Daughter of Jerusalem! See, your king comes to you, righteous and having salvation, gentle and riding on a donkey, on a colt, the foal of a donkey." Jesus did this deliberately. He was pointing his disciples and the entire multitude to this prophecy and was thus also making a statement for us and all men to heed today. His riding into Jerusalem on a donkey's colt also demonstrated that he was not a Messiah in the political sense, as his disciples and so many others hoped, but the humble servant of his heavenly Father. Jesus chose to ride on the colt, even as the prophecy had stated. When they brought the colt to Jesus, the disciples threw their cloaks on the colt to serve as a comfortable "saddle."

What was the reaction of the crowd? It was made up of those who had been with Jesus almost the entire day and also such who hearing he was present (see John 11:56; 12:12,13) came out to meet him. They scattered their cloaks on the path where Jesus would ride and welcomed him as their king, even as the followers of Jehu had once welcomed him (see 2 Kings 9:13). The scattering of palm branches (see John 12:13) and other foliage (see Matthew 21:8) in his path was patterned on the words of Psalm 118:27: "With boughs in hand, join in the festal procession up to the horns of the altar." Jesus' entry into Jerusalem was a triumphal procession, although at the moment most of the crowd did not know that his real triumph would come later that week when he would conquer sin and death.

The words with which the crowd welcomed Jesus tell us even more about our Savior. Most of these words (and the four Evangelists naturally give different statements, for the crowd must have numbered in the thousands) are taken from Psalm 118:25,26: "O LORD, save us; O LORD, grant us success. Blessed is he who comes in the name of the LORD." To come in the Lord's name means to come carrying out his plan of salvation. That indeed was Jesus' assignment, although the crowd did not know it. Speaking of him as the coming one is also understood messianically in Scripture: "The scepter will not depart from Judah, nor the ruler's staff from between his feet, until he comes to whom it belongs and the obedience of the nations is his" (Genesis 49:10). Even more plain is Zechariah 9:9 quoted just previously. Read also Psalm 40:6-8, applied to Christ in Hebrews 10:5-10, and Malachi 3:1. The first to recognize him as such were Mary and Joseph, Simeon and Anna. The first to proclaim his coming was John the Baptist (see Mark 1:7; Luke 3:15-18; John 3:31).

The next words of the crowd, as quoted by Mark, reveal still another facet concerning who Jesus is: "Blessed is the coming kingdom of our father David." These words point to Jesus as king, even as the crowd explicitly said according to John 12:13: "Blessed is the King of Israel." Jesus is the messianic king not just because he was a descendant of David — many of his descendants did not become kings —but because he is that king of David's line whom God promised. "For to us a child is born, to us a son is given, and the government will be on his shoulders. And he will be called Wonderful Counselor, Mighty God, Everlasting Father, Prince of Peace. Of the increase of his government and peace there will be no end. He will reign on David's throne and over his kingdom, establishing and upholding it with justice and righteousness from that time on and forever" (Isaiah 9:6,7). Read also Psalm 132:11 and Jeremiah 23:5. Jesus wants the deeds and the words of Palm Sunday also to march right into our hearts, so that we too may acknowledge him for what he is.

The triumphal march very likely began late in the forenoon and lasted late into the afternoon. Then our Lord and his disciples finally came to the temple, Jesus' Father's house. Only Mark recorded that the cleansing of the temple actually took place on the next day, Monday. The other Evangelists did not designate the day, but joined the temple incident with the triumphal march into Jerusalem, because both demonstrated the royal power of our Lord. That's why Matthew also did not divide the cursing and withering of the fig tree into two sections on two days as Mark did. On Palm Sunday our Lord late in the day did inspect the temple in preparation for its cleansing the following day. In the meantime, since it was crowded and probably unsafe for Jesus and his disciples to remain in Jerusalem overnight (see John 11:49-57), they went and stayed with friends in Bethany, or camped out.

Jesus Clears the Temple

¹²The next day as they were leaving Bethany, Jesus was hungry. ¹³Seeing in the distance a fig tree in leaf, he went to find out if it had any fruit. When he reached it, he found nothing but leaves, because it was not the season for figs. ¹⁴Then he said to the tree, "May no one ever eat fruit from you again." And his disciples heard him say it.

¹⁵On reaching Jerusalem, Jesus entered the temple area and began driving out those who were buying and selling there. He overturned the tables of the money changers and the benches of those selling doves, ¹⁶and would not allow anyone to carry mer-

chandise through the temple courts. ¹⁷And as he taught them, he said, "Is it not written: 'My house will be called a house of prayer for all nations'? But you have made it 'a den of robbers.' "

¹⁸The chief priests and teachers of the law heard this and began looking for a way to kill him, for they feared him, because the whole crowd was amazed at his teaching.

¹⁹When evening came, they went out of the city.

(Matthew 21:12-19; Luke 19:45-48)

Matthew and Luke in relating the events of Holy Week connect Jesus' triumphal entry into Jerusalem with his cleansing of the temple, since both events reveal the authority of Jesus the Messiah. When Matthew then relates what happened to the fig tree, he relates it as one event instead of dividing it into two episodes as Mark does. Mark relates it as it happened chronologically. He divides the account of the fig tree. In the first, Jesus used the event to deepen the understanding of the disciples for what immediately followed, the temple being cleansed because it was misused and thus did not bring forth the fruits the Lord God desired.

On Palm Sunday evening Jesus and the Twelve had gone out to Bethany. Early the next morning they returned to Jerusalem. Having left without breakfast, Jesus was hungry. In the distance alongside the road and thus ownerless was a fig tree in full leaf. Since the leaves usually followed gradually upon the setting of the first figs, Jesus had every right to expect the tree would have figs suitable for eating. (Notice here Jesus did not use his supernatural knowledge as at other times.) When he came to the tree, he found nothing but leaves — a promise, but no fulfillment. It was then that Jesus pronounced the curse on the fig tree.

The words seem harsh. Was Jesus taking out his frustration on the tree? Not so. The disciples heard Jesus' words. used the tree as a lesson to prepare his disciples for what was to happen next in the temple. Then the next morning he applied it to their own ministry and life. He let them know that by having blessed them he had the right to expect fruit from them in due season.

By cleansing the temple Jesus publicly brought to the attention of God's people that those in authority (the priests and the Sanhedrin) had been desecrating the house of God. In order to bring their sacrifices the worshipers according to the Mosaic Law had to offer animals that were ceremonially clean. To pay the temple tax pilgrims also had to have an opportunity to exchange their foreign currency for some that was acceptable (compare Mark 12:16 with Exodus 20:4). But this should not have been done in a temple area, that is, in the court of the Gentiles. That was the only place in the temple where the Gentiles could gather to say their prayers, to hear God's word and to meditate. This became almost impossible in a place filled with animals, animal sounds and animal smells in addition to the clink of coins and cries of the money changers. What made it even worse was all these concessions controlled by the temple authorities made charges that were exorbitant. The Gentiles were robbed of the one place in the temple where their prayers were acceptable to God. It had become a place of merchandising. The situation cried to heaven for remedy. All the more so since Christ had three years before (see John 2:13-17) also cleansed the temple. His action of that time had not been taken to heart; the evils, with full approval of the authorities, had taken over again. So Jesus in his zeal for the house of his Father again took a hand in restoring it to a God-pleasing condition. At least it stayed that way for the rest of Holy Week, since Jesus daily came back there to teach the people.

He cleaned out the court of the Gentiles — by driving out those selling and buying, by overturning the tables of the money changers and those selling doves — with his authoritative word. None had an answer for his righteous anger; their consciences agreed. Then he also prevented anyone from using the court of the Gentiles as a shortcut between the eastern section of Jerusalem and the Mount of Olives. Those in authority, who had permitted this, had lost all sense of the presence of God. Strange as it may seem, this prohibition also was included in the Jewish Talmud.

When quiet had been restored, Jesus enlarged on the words he had spoken in driving out those who bought and sold by calling attention to what they had ignored — God's own written word. First, he cited a prophet: "And foreigners who bind themselves to the LORD ... these I will bring to my holy mountain and give them joy in my house of prayer. Their burnt offerings and sacrifices will be accepted on my altar; for my house will be called a house of prayer for all nations"(Isaiah 56:6,7). Then he proceeded to quote another prophet: "Has this house, which bears my Name, become a den of robbers to you? But I have been watching! declares the LORD" (Jeremiah 7:11). The temple officials had not only robbed God of the honor due him, but also the Gentiles of their only place in the temple to meet God. To such depths the official religion had fallen in Christ's day. God's house had become a hangout for such who put their own advantage above the Lord's will and other people's good.

Jesus' actions here also remind us of our own relationship to him and his Word. "For if God did not spare the natural branches, he will not spare you either"(Romans 11:21). Do we take our faith and our church life seriously? Or has our church life deteriorated to no more than just a social get-together?

The reaction of the priests and members of the Sanhedrin was the very opposite of what God looked for, thus a complete justification of our Lord's action. The religious leaders saw in Jesus no more than a rival invading their territory. They were afraid because the crowds listening to Jesus' teaching were beginning to recognize it as the truth. That's why the chief priests and teachers of the law began to look for a way to put Jesus to death. Little did they realize God would use their envy and hatred to bring Jesus to the sacrificial cross. Did any of them ever repent? In their midst there were indeed such who did not side with the leaders, people like Nicodemus, Joseph of Arimathea and others (see John 12:42). But they did not go public with their faith until Good Friday or after our Lord's ascension and particularly after Pentecost. However the majority did not repent and by this action wrote their own verdict. What a warning!

That evening Jesus and the Twelve again left Jerusalem.

The Withered Fig Tree

20In the morning, as they went along, they saw the fig tree withered from the roots. 21Peter remembered and said to Jesus, "Rabbi, look! The fig tree you cursed has withered!"

22"Have faith in God," Jesus answered. 23"I tell you the truth, if anyone says to this mountain, 'Go, throw yourself into the sea,' and does not doubt in his heart but believes that what he says will happen, it will be done for him. 24Therefore I tell you, whatever you ask for in prayer, believe that you will receive it, and it will be yours. 25And when you stand praying, if you hold anything against anyone, forgive him, so that your Father in heaven may forgive you your sins."

(Matthew 21:20-22)

On their way back to Jerusalem on Tuesday morning Jesus and his disciples again passed the fig tree. By this time it was totally withered from the roots up. Jesus' judgment was irrevocable. It was Peter who first called attention to the tree. All the other disciples also marveled at how quickly

159

the tree had withered (see Matthew 21:20). Undoubtedly they were also reminded of the words Jesus had said about backsliding Israel and its unbelieving leaders.

When asked about the withered fig tree, the Lord did not reply directly to the question, but applied what had happened to his disciples and their faith. Israel's leaders had fallen from faith. Jesus did not want that to happen to the disciples. Since they were near the Mount of Olives and not far from the Dead Sea, Jesus used the examples of a mountain and a sea to teach his disciples about faith. It can move mountains, as Jesus stated.

Faith is implicit reliance, trust and confidence in God's promises, even if they seem as impossible as a mountain throwing itself into a sea. God after all is almighty. Of course God has nowhere promised to answer our prayer if we were to pray that a mountain be tossed into the sea. To know what he has promised, we must study his holy Word. Therefore our faith and the prayers it speaks, too often reciting simply our needs and desires which are usually gigantic, are to be based on what God has promised.

Jesus also called attention to an element that can completely undermine any prayer we bring to the throne of God. A heart filled with ill-will against others is not acceptable to God. The temple cleansing had revealed that the religious leaders in Israel were people with such hearts. The prayers they were addressing to God were as false as their hearts were evil and would not be answered.

Nor does Jesus say that we should be ready to forgive only when asked for pardon. We are to forgive even before being asked. That is how faith, true faith, acts. This is meant not only for the Twelve, but for all of us.

Verse 26 in the King James Version is only in a footnote in the NIV Bible because it is not in some of the oldest manuscripts. We are, however, not losers because of that.

Verse 26 would add nothing new here; it is simply the negative of verse 25. Besides, we find exactly the same words in Jesus' Sermon on the Mount (see Matthew 6:15).

The Authority of Jesus Questioned

²⁷They arrived again in Jerusalem, and while Jesus was walking in the temple courts, the chief priests, the teachers of the law and the elders came to him. ²⁸"By what authority are you doing these things?" they asked. "And who gave you authority to do this?" ²⁹Jesus replied, "I will ask you one question. Answer me, and I will tell you by what authority I am doing these things. ³⁰John's baptism — was it from heaven, or from men? Tell me!"

³¹They discussed it among themselves and said, "If we say, 'From heaven,' he will ask, 'Then why didn't you believe him?' ³²But if we say, 'From men' . . . " (They feared the people, for everyone held that John really was a prophet.)

³³So they answered Jesus, "We don't know."

Jesus said, "Neither will I tell you by what authority I am doing these things."

(Matthew 21:23-27; Luke 20:1-8)

On Tuesday of Holy Week the Lord spent a great part of the morning teaching in the temple and preaching the good news to the people that gathered there (see Luke 20:1). During a break he was approached by a delegation from the Sanhedrin. Their purpose was not aboveboard (v 18). Christ knew that. As members of the Sanhedrin they had not only the right but also the duty to ask by what authority Christ was doing things such as clearing the temple. However they had already made up their mind about Jesus (see 3:22; 7:5; 8:11; 10:2). Although their question seemed harmless, they were actually seeking an answer whereby they could either ridicule him before the people or accuse him of blasphemy — the very charge they later brought against him (see 14:63,64).

161

Jesus avoided the trap they laid for him and by means of his counter question gave them an answer they could not misunderstand. He asked them about John's baptism — to be understood is his entire ministry — whether it was from God or from men. They had from the very start made up their minds about John by rejecting his baptism for themselves (see Luke 7:30). In their hearts they rejected both John and Jesus as sent by God.

Jesus' question placed them between a rock and a hard place. They knew John the Baptist in his preaching and teaching had pointed to Jesus as the Christ (see John 3:28), so that whatever they would now say about John would also apply to Jesus. If they would say, "From heaven," they knew Jesus would ask, "Why didn't you believe him?" that is, also believe what he said of me. Since the people accepted John as a prophet, they feared the crowd would stone them (see Luke 20:6) if they were to answer "From men." So they answered, "We don't know." The chief priests, teachers of the law and the elders pleaded the fifth amendment thereby condemning themselves. They refused to face the truth of God's word, which John had cited as support for his own ministry, which Jesus had proclaimed in his preaching and attested by his miracles, and which they themselves had vowed to teach and proclaim. How sad! Christ here gave them the opportunity to repent and confess, but they wanted none of it. They rejected the Savior because they valued their positions more highly than their salvation.

The Holy Spirit by having Mark record their questions and that of Christ faces us with these questions also. What is our answer? May it be the answer Peter gave, "You are the Christ".

The Parable of the Tenants

12 He then began to speak to them in parables: "A man planted a vineyard. He put a wall around it, dug a pit for the winepress and built a watchtower. Then he rented the vineyard to some farmers and went away on a journey. ²At harvest time he sent a servant to the tenants to collect from them some of the fruit of the vineyard. ³But they seized him, beat him and sent him away empty-handed. ⁴Then he sent another servant to them; they struck this man on the head and treated him shamefully. ⁵He sent still another, and that one they killed. He sent many others; some of them they beat, others they killed

⁶"He had one left to send, a son, whom he loved. He sent him last of all, saying, 'They will respect my son.'

⁷"But the tenants said to one another, 'This is the heir. Come, let's kill him, and the inheritance will be ours.' ⁸So they took him and killed him, and threw him out of the vineyard.

⁹"What then will the owner of the vineyard do? He will come and kill those tenants and give the vineyard to others. ¹⁰Haven't you read this scripture:

" 'The stone the builders rejected
has become the capstone;
¹¹the Lord has done this,
and it is marvelous in our eyes'?"

¹²Then they looked for a way to arrest him because they knew he had spoken the parable against them. But they were afraid of the crowd; so they left him and went away.

(Matthew 21:33-46; Luke 20:9-19)

When the delegation from the Sanhedrin refused to answer Jesus' question, he too would not give them a direct answer. Instead, he gave them a veiled answer by means of a parable which he immediately spoke to them and to the crowd around them.

A parable is a story using common, ordinary things or situations from daily life in order to teach a spiritual truth. During his ministry our Lord spoke many parables (chapter 4), and during Holy Week he also taught by means of parables, as Mark indicates and the other Evangelists also record. Parables as a rule make only one point. This particular parable is different. For us of the New Testament it is practically self-explanatory.

The religious leaders of Israel also got the point. It gave them not only the answer to their question, "By what authority are you doing these things?" It was also a vivid follow-up to the cleansing of the temple and a blunt warning concerning their own fate if they did not repent.

Jesus used as an illustration a situation common in that day, tenant farmers and absentee landlords. Unlike other parables this was also a take-off on a passage familiar to all who knew their Old Testament (see Isaiah 5:1-7). As in the Isaiah passage so here too the vineyard was Israel and the owner was God himself. But as he continued, Jesus developed the parable to fit the present situation. The servants sent to collect the fruit were the prophets sent to Israel throughout the Old Testament era (see v 5 and Matthew 21:34-36). The last of these was John the Baptist. The prophet's pleas and their divine messages usually fell on deaf ears. Some were persecuted, others killed (see 2 Chronicles 24:20-22). Zechariah was a prophet, but not the writer of the book by that name). The son in the parable was none other than Jesus himself. He called himself the "son, whom he loved." He was therefore greater than the prophets and was the one who would bring them God's final word.

God showed incredible grace and inexhaustible patience in his dealings with Israel. Who of us would have sent his son under circumstances like this? Jesus also pictured the unbelievable hard-heartedness and stubborn unbelief of the chosen people, especially of their political and religious leaders. Not only were these already facts in the days of the Old Testament, but they were open and blatant throughout Jesus' entire ministry. There was no excuse for that.

Jesus said that the vineyard had everything needed to produce an abundant harvest. Israel had God's word; it had his temple. But it had made of God's law a method of earning heaven. So when Jesus came to his own people, they would not receive him, except a very few who were waiting for the redemption in Israel. Israel's leaders saw him only as a competitor. They rejected him as the son and heir and then put him to death outside the walls of Jerusalem. They inflicted the ultimate dishonor by crucifying him between two malefactors. Though Pilate ordered the actual crucifixion, Israel's leaders were basically the guilty ones.

What Jesus here said that the tenants would do with the son and heir had not as yet taken place although it would happen a few days later. That makes these words not only a warning but also a plea to repent. He proceeded to tell them what would happen to them if they would go through with their evil plans and would not heed his plea. Christ's question was to the point: "What then will the owner of the vineyard do?" The answer was: "He will come and kill those tenants and give the vineyard to others." That was exactly what happened when Israel's religious leaders rejected Christ, put him to death, and then persisted in their impenitence. The vineyard was turned over to the Christian church.

Today we are both the recipients and the caretakers of God's saving word. Pray God that we may never reject or decimate that good news of Jesus Christ and thus also forfeit the blessing!

In telling this parable Jesus did not stop with the killing of the beloved son nor with the owner's judgment on the tenants. He next indicated that the final outcome for himself would not be death. He would rise again; yes, he would become the capstone of the building which would be the new Israel. Therewith he called his hearers' attention to the words of Psalm 118:22,23, the same words the multitude had used in welcoming him on Palm Sunday.

The chief priests, the teachers of the law and the elders recognized that the parable was meant for them. But they did not heed Jesus' words and repent. Rather, they looked for ways to arrest Jesus as soon as possible. The only thing that stopped them for the moment was their fear of the crowd, who approved of Jesus' words even if it did not fully understand them. And this was not the end of their efforts to ensnare Jesus in his own words in order to give them an excuse to arrest and execute him.

Paying Taxes to Caesar

13Later they sent some of the Pharisees and Herodians to Jesus to catch him in his words. 14They came to him and said, "Teacher, we know you are a man of integrity. You aren't swayed by men, because you pay no attention to who they are; but you teach the way of God in accordance with the truth. Is it right to pay taxes to Caesar or not? 15Should we pay or shouldn't we?"

But Jesus knew their hypocrisy. "Why are you trying to trap me?" he asked. "Bring me a denarius and let me look at it." 16They brought him the coin, and he asked them, "Whose portrait is this? And whose inscription?"

"Caesar's," they replied.

17Then Jesus said to them, "Give to Caesar what is Caesar's and to God what is God's."

And they were amazed at him.

(Matthew 22:15-22; Luke 20:20-26)

Although the delegation from the Sanhedrin left, nevertheless they were determined to keep their eyes and ears open in order, if possible, to trap Jesus in his own words. Later that day they made another attempt. The Pharisees sent some of their own disciples as religious spies and some supporters of Herod Antipas as political spies to question Jesus (see Matthew 22:16). The Pharisees hated Herod, but they were ready to make common cause with his followers if thereby they could get the better of Jesus. Herod and Pilate later also became friends (see Luke 23:12). When they came to Jesus, his enemies sought to disarm him with flattering words. Strange, but what they said about Christ was the absolute truth; only they didn't believe a word of it.

The tax they inquired about was the poll tax that each individual had to pay annually. The Jews hated it and suspected that perhaps Christ did too. It was a known fact that even one of Jesus' own disciples had previously belonged to the party of the Zealots (see 3:18). After all, why should God's people pay tax to a pagan emperor?

Jesus saw through their deceit and asked them outright, "Why are you trying to trap me?" His next words, "Bring me a denarius and let me look at it," are somewhat ironic. Had he never seen the coin? That they had such a coin in their possession and immediately offered it to him demonstrated their hypocrisy. They had been making use of it all along.

The denarius was a small silver coin which bore the emperor's bust on one side and on the other the following inscription: "Tiberius Caesar Augustus, son of the divine Augustus" — naturally in Latin. The Pharisees made use of it in paying their taxes. Thus they tacitly acknowledged Caesar's authority and really answered their own question. Jesus could have stopped right there.

However this time, unlike the other time when they had asked, "By what authority do you do these things?"Jesus gave them an answer. It was an answer with which neither the Romans could find fault nor the Pharisees nor the Herodians.

This answer holds good to our own day. "Give to Caesar what is Caesar's and to God what is God's." Both the state and the church have their separate domains, and to both we must give their respective tribute. The state is also a divine institution and is used by God for his purpose. The decision we must make is to determine what belongs to which.

Perhaps this is a section which will help us face the differences we find between the various Gospels. Read Mark 12:13-17, Matthew 22:15-22 and Luke 20:20-26. The Evangelists report the words of Jesus and the details of the account itself a bit differently. Does that question the absolute truth and inspiration of the Scriptures? Details frequently differ. One Evangelist may zero in on the deeds of the persons involved. Another may stress all the persons involved and what they say. But note that neither the one nor the other rules out the others. Consequently there is really no disagreement.

Jesus spoke Aramaic as a rule, and the writers of the New Testament wrote in Greek. In translating we need not always use the same word to express the same truth. That is even evident in translating from Greek into English. The English vocabulary and sentence structure used by the NIV need not be identical with the KJV. When, for example, the NIV in verse 15 uses "asked" and the KJV uses "said unto them," neither is in error, for what Jesus said was a question. Likewise, when the NIV translates "Jesus" instead of "him" in verses 13 and 15, or "coin" instead of "it" in verse 16, or "replied" instead of "said unto him" in verse 16, that is done for the sake of clearness. However if anything were added that contradicts the original Greek, that would be a different matter.

Besides, we must remember that while the Greek text of the New Testament was inspired, the English and the German translations are not. But we know that, whether we use Luther's German or the KJV or the NIV, there are very few translations we may properly question. God does not demand that all of us use only the original Hebrew and Greek. In the New Testament many Old Testament quotations are quoted from the Septuagint, the Greek translation of the Hebrew Old Testament. Yet it is the Holy Spirit himself who quotes, even though at times the translation may technically not agree with the original Hebrew text. In using translations, unless it can be demonstrated that they are false and contradict other statements of Scripture, we are still using God's Word.

Marriage at the Resurrection

[18]Then the Sadducees, who say there is no resurrection, came to him with a question. [19]"Teacher," they said, "Moses wrote for us that if a man's brother dies and leaves a wife but no children, the man must marry the widow and have children for his brother. [20]Now there were seven brothers. The first one married and died without leaving any children. [21]The second one married the widow, but he also died, leaving no child. It was the same with the third. [22]In fact, none of the seven left any children. Last of all, the woman died too. [23]At the resurrection whose wife will she be, since the seven were married to her?"

[24]Jesus replied, "Are you not in error because you do not know the Scriptures or the power of God? [25]When the dead rise, they will neither marry nor be given in marriage; they will be like the angels of heaven. [26]Now about the dead rising — have you not read in the book of Moses, in the account of the bush, how God said to him, 'I am the God of Abraham, the God of Isaac, and the God of Jacob'? [27]He is not the God of the dead, but of the living. You are badly mistaken!"

(Matthew 22:23-33; Luke 20:27-40)

It was a day when our Lord could hardly turn about without being challenged with questions. His answers were supplied from his thorough knowledge of the Scriptures. The Bible is indeed for us the source of our answers to the questions of life. It is especially "a lamp to my feet and a light for my path" (Psalm 119:105), so that we may overcome the attacks of Satan and rejoice fully in the grace and love of God.

This time it was the Sadducees who came to Jesus with a question they felt convinced would embarrass him and cause the people to question his authority. Mark tells what their basic theological error was. The Sadducees "say there is no resurrection," and thus no life after death — no eternal judgment, no angels or devils, perhaps even no soul. They accepted only the writings of Moses as authentic Scriptures.

Many of the modernists and liberals of our day also deny the resurrection, especially the resurrection of Christ. They should not really be called modernists, since that false doctrine has been around for a long time. However the ancient Sadducees were more orthodox than their modern counterparts, for they still taught that Moses wrote the Pentateuch, a fact which the liberals of today simply do not accept.

The Sadducees did not refer to Moses' words (see Deuteronomy 25:5,6) to question or ridicule Moses' regulation concerning levirate marriage (they seemed to accept that), but rather to ridicule any doctrine of a resurrection. Why? Because Jesus had just spoken about the resurrection, though indirectly. In the parable of the vineyard he had told the delegation from the Sanhedrin that though the tenants would kill "the son," or the builders reject "the stone," yet he would become "the capstone," thus not remain dead but rise again. Their question, "At the resurrection whose wife will she be, since the seven were married to her?" was meant to ridicule any possibility of a physical resurrection.

Jesus didn't enter in on their question, but rather zeroed in on the underlying errors — their ignorance of Scripture and their ignorance of the power of God. He told them that concerning the resurrection they had not taken into consideration the fact the former laws regulating life here on earth will no longer apply. There will be no marriage. Since there will be no death, there will be no need to propagate.

Then he added, since they also denied the existence of angels, that in the resurrection human beings "will be like the angels in heaven." Though our actual bodies will rise, they will be transformed, made perfect instruments of the spirit. Read 1 Corinthians 15:42-44 and note particularly that the persons being transformed are the identical persons who lived and died here on earth. Paul says, "*We* will be changed" (1 Corinthians 15:52).

The Old Testament also teaches the resurrection of the dead, although not in as much detail as the New Testament. Read Isaiah 26:19 and Daniel 12:2. Genesis 22:5 also shows Abraham's faith in God's power to bring the dead — his own son whom he had been commanded to sacrifice — back to life.

In answering the Sadducees Jesus quoted from the Pentateuch, because the Sadducees did accept the books of Moses. His reference to Exodus 3:2 as "in the account of the bush" made it easier for the hearers to locate Jesus' specific quotation. In the days of Jesus here on earth the Old Testament had not yet been divided into chapters and verses for ease of reference.

Jesus told them that they had not properly understood the passage. God said, "I am the God of Abraham, . . . " and not, "I was." Abraham, Isaac and Jacob at the time of Christ were alive in God's presence even though they had died centuries before (see Luke 20:37,38). Since God is the God of the living, that also involves the resurrection of the body at the end of time. God does not permit death to destroy his covenant.

This would be proved in a very special way less than a week later when our Lord Jesus would rise from the dead. God's promise of the resurrection and eternal life may transcend our understanding, but since it is his promise we will comfort ourselves with it in life and death and as we face the

171

last day. Though my body must be transformed and made fit for heaven, I will be the same person who was accepted by the Lord in the sacrament of Holy Baptism when he declared me his child and heir. Jesus' answer to the Sadducees of old helps us overcome the arguments of today's Sadducees.

The Greatest Commandment

28One of the teachers of the law came and heard them debating. Noticing that Jesus had given them a good answer, he asked him, "Of all the commandments, which is the most important?"

29"The most important one," answered Jesus, "is this: 'Hear, O Israel, the Lord our God, the Lord is one. 30Love the Lord your God with all your heart and with all your soul and with all your mind and with all your strength.' 31The second is this: 'Love your neighbor as yourself.' There is no commandment greater than these."

32"Well said, teacher," the man replied. "You are right in saying that God is one and there is no other but him. 33To love him with all your heart, with all your understanding and with all your strength, and to love your neighbor as yourself is more important than all burnt offerings and sacrifices."

34When Jesus saw that he had answered wisely, he said to him, "You are not far from the kingdom of God." And from then on no one dared ask him any more questions.

(Matthew 22:34-40)

Pleased in spite of themselves that Christ had given the Sadducees a theologically good answer and silenced them (see Matthew 22:46), the Pharisees made a final attempt to catch Jesus in his words. Their spokesman, this time an expert in the law, put a question to Christ that traditionally had been a point of contention among the Pharisees themselves. That's understandable, since they had subdivided and expanded God's commandments into 613 ordinances.

Naturally some of them were bound to be considered more important than others. The question was: "Of all the commandments, which is the most important?"

Christ found no difficulty in answering. God's will has to do with man's relationship to God and with man's relationship to man. The answer therefore must be clear from Scripture. It is. Jesus quoted Deuteronomy 6:4,5 and Leviticus 19:18. That God was spoken of here as "one" does not undermine the doctrine of the Trinity, for what was spoken of here was the oneness of being (essence), not of person. Remember also that the Old Testament used the plural in reference to the one God (see Genesis 1:26). Since there is only one God — when God is called *Jehovah* he is the God of grace, and when God is called *Elohim* he is the God of might and power — God rightly demands that we love him with all our heart, with all our soul, with all our mind and with all our strength. This by the way was a very familiar passage for Old Testament believers, since it was part of the prayer all pious Israelites were expected to pray three times a day. There was no doubt in their estimation that this was the most important commandment. What was new about Jesus' answer was that he placed the commandment, "Love your neighbor as yourself," on the same level with the other saying, "There is no commandment greater than these."

It's easy to say we love God above everyone and everything, but the proof of it usually becomes visible in our actions towards our fellowmen whoever they are. We are to love them as much as ourselves thereby excluding all selfishness. Clearly this "love" goes far beyond "like." One's heart cannot be right with God if it is not right with one's fellowmen.

The teacher of the law simply could not disagree with Christ. In fact, he wholeheartedly stated his approval of Jesus' answer. He showed it by repeating Jesus' words and by elaborating on them. He agreed that loving God and loving the neighbor are more important than all burnt offerings and sacrifices, most of which simply indicate repentance for sins against God's laws. He recalled 1 Samuel 15:22 and Hosea 6:6 and remembered how easily ritual can take the place of love.

His words are a reminder for us not to let our worship services become something that simply goes in one ear and out the other, but that we are to put into practice what we hear.

The words of this teacher of the law also show he was drawn to Christ. Jesus was pleased with the man's answer, particularly when he compared it with the deafening silence that had so often greeted his statements. When Jesus now said to this man, "You are not far from the kingdom of God," he thereby let the man know that he had truly recognized the ethical nature of the kingdom of God. Jesus' words were both a challenge and an invitation. He challenged him to take the next step and invited him to believe in Christ as his Savior. Did the man take that step? We don't know, but it is not ruled out. Jesus' words are powerful.

This then was the final queston directed to Jesus by the enemies of our Lord. By using the Scriptures Jesus always came out the winner. Yet in spite of that they rejected him. Faith is not a matter of winning an argument, but a gift of God which however can be rejected. It was to save them from this dire result that Jesus now in turn asked them a question and issued a warning.

A Question and a Warning

35While Jesus was teaching in the temple courts, he asked, "How is it that the teachers of the law say that the Christ is the son of David? 36David himself, speaking by the Holy Spirit, declared: 'The Lord said to my Lord: Sit at my right hand until I put your

enemies under your feet.' ³⁷David himself calls him 'Lord.' How then can he be his son?"

The large crowd listened to him with delight.

³⁸As he taught, Jesus said, "Watch out for the teachers of the law. They like to walk around in flowing robes and be greeted in the marketplaces, ³⁹and have the most important seats in the synagogues and the places of honor at banquets. ⁴⁰They devour widows' houses and for a show make lengthy prayers. Such men will be punished most severely."

(Matthew 22:41-46; 23:1-7; Luke 20:41-47)

This was our Lord's final public teaching before his passion. The opponents of Jesus no longer raised any questions; they had found it impossible to trap him in his statements. There was only one thing left for them — arrest and kill Jesus, "but not during the Feast or there may be a riot among the people" (Matthew 26:5). They would not be able to adhere to their own timetable; God had chosen the time and the place.

Jesus had some last words directed both to them (see Matthew 22:41) and to the crowd (12:37). He took up the point that enraged the Pharisees above all and asked, "Who is Christ?" Jesus had already given them his answer when he had asked them about the baptism of John and when he had spoken of himself as the "son, whom he loved" in the Parable of the Tenants. Now he came back to that very point, for unless he is the very Son of God he cannot be the Messiah, the Christ, the Savior.

Jesus began by referring to what they had said and then turning to Scripture. The teachers of the law taught that the Christ was the son of David, a mere human messiah and no more. Jesus was indeed a descendant of David as genealogies in Matthew 1 and Luke 3 state. By teaching that the Christ was the son of David, the teachers of the law only expected the messianic kingdom to be an earthly restoration of Israel's former glory. Jesus pointed out that they had not really heeded the Scriptures. After citing Psalm 110:1, he added the pertinent question they should have asked themselves, a question that allowed for only one answer: "David himself calls him 'Lord.' How then can he be his son?" The only proper answer is that Christ is both: the eternal Son of the Father — thus God, and also a descendant of David —thus man. The Pharisees were ready to acknowledge the latter, but not the former. They were ready to make use of him as the son of David, but not ready to welcome him as their divine Lord and Savior.

In doing so they rejected the Scriptures which Jesus says David wrote "by the Holy Spirit," that is, by inspiration. That is Jesus' own view of the Scriptures. And it is because of words like these from the mouth of Jesus Christ and other direct statements in the Scriptures that we accept the Bible as God's inspired and inerrant Word. Through the Scriptures the Lord strengthens our weak flesh to overcome sins such as those Jesus calls attention to in his next words, when he exposes these teachers of the law for what they really are.

It was no mean honor to have been a teacher of the law. We have already learned from the words of Christ (9:33-37) that as a Christian pastor or teacher today our life is to be a life of service to others, not of lording it over them and taking advantage of them. Jesus pointed out the hypocrisy of his opponents. They wore flowing robes in the marketplaces to evoke honorable greetings. They had seats up front in the synagogues and thus were highly visible and near the ark that contained the sacred scrolls. And of course they took the places of honor at banquets. Self-centered pride! But there was an even darker side. They took advantage of widows in their poverty and then covered up their wickedness by saying long prayers so that everyone would think them to be holy. Many more examples are given in Matthew 23:1-36.

They may have been able to fool men, but not God. "Such men will be punished most severely," says David's son and David's Lord, the one who will judge them on the last day. And of that judgment he would speak very shortly in private with his disciples.

The Widow's Offering

⁴¹Jesus sat down opposite the place where the offerings were put and watched the crowd putting their money into the temple treasury. Many rich people threw in large amounts. ⁴²But a poor widow came and put in two very small copper coins, worth only a fraction of a penny.

⁴³Calling his disciples to him, Jesus said, "I tell you the truth, this poor widow has put more into the treasury than all the others. ⁴⁴They all gave out of their wealth; but she, out of her poverty, put in everything — all she had to live on."

(Luke 21:1-4)

These were Jesus' last moments in the temple — strange that he should spend them sitting in the court of the women, where the offerings were deposited into thirteen trumpet-shaped receptacles. Jesus, the Son of God, was reading the hearts of the worshipers.

He also examines the hearts of all today who confess, "I believe in God, the Father, . . . and in Jesus Christ, his only Son, our Lord." Do we mean it? Do our offerings of time, talents and money prove it? Offerings are often the real test of faith.

Many rich people gave much. Jesus did not say their gifts were not welcome or not needed. What he did want his disciples and us to note is that our gifts are acceptable only if they come from hearts filled with love and trust. That was true of this widow in a very special way.

That she was a widow makes this final episode in the temple dramatic and stirring. Jesus had just spoken to the teachers of the law who "devour widows' houses." Were some of these among the rich who gave much? We are not told.

What the woman gave, of course, was very little in comparison with what the rich gave. It amounted to "two very small copper coins, worth only a fraction of a penny." We have no equivalent in our currency. The copper coin was called a *lepton*, meaning "small, thin, light." The two were worth one half a *kodrantes*. This in turn was worth one sixty-fourth of a *denarius*, the daily wage of a laborer in those days. Since laborers then did not earn as much as they do today, her offering was indeed a tiny amount.

Here the Greek uses the word *kodrantes*, which is a transliteration of the Latin *quadrans*. Mark often transliterates Latin terms in the Greek text of his Gospel. This is an indication that his Gospel was written for Roman Christians and possibly in Rome.

The widow's gift was not tiny in the eyes of Christ. Calling together his disciples — they had a lesson to learn even as we do — he told them that this widow had put in more than all the others. He knew this, not because he had asked her, but because he as the Son of God could look into her heart. Jesus knows vastly more about us and all others than we know about ourselves.

Why did Jesus say that her gift was "more ... than all the others"? Unlike the rich, who had more than enough left over, she gave all she had. This was an act of worship, of love, of faith and of absolute trust. And finally that is what it means to be a disciple.

The Lord measures our gifts by the spirit in which they are given. He does not with these words ask us to empty our bank accounts, but he invites us to give him ourselves. Then our gifts to his treasury will also be liberal, and our life will become a life of true stewardship.

This event is particularly thrilling because we know the rest of the story. This was Jesus' last visit to the temple. From here he went forward to offer himself — all that he is — on the cross to pay the price we could not pay, to make the contribution we could not make. On Good Friday he paid the entire debt and for the moment became even poorer than this poor widow.

The Discourse on the Mount of Olives

Most of what Jesus tells us in Mark 13 still lies in the future. Some is part of our present situation — contempt and persecution; some is of the past — the destruction of the temple and Jerusalem. However when Jesus spoke these words to his disciples, the destruction was still in the future. The very fact it took place is a pledge of assurance that all Jesus said here will most certainly be fulfilled. His words in this chapter were spoken so that we too might constantly be on the alert. Jesus even included us in the last verse of this chapter when he said, "What I say to you [the disciples], I say to everyone: 'Watch!' " This was not the first time that Jesus spoke about the end of this age and about eternity. See 3:29; 4:29; 8:38; 9:47; 10:30 and 12:25-27. Then look ahead to 14:25,62 and 16:16.

We must be careful not to misuse these words of our Lord. They are meant to equip us to live and bear witness to Christ in a world that is hostile to the Christian message. They are not meant to satisfy our natural curiosity about the date of judgment day. That is known only to the heavenly Father (13:32).

These words of our Lord speak of only one second coming of Christ (13:26,27) on judgment day. This guards against the false interpretation of Revelation 20 so prevalent

179

in many churches today that at the end of the world Christ
will come twice — the first time a thousand years before the
end to establish a millennial kingdom with its capital at
Jerusalem and the second time on judgment day. Noting the
words of this chapter and studying carefully the words of
Revelation 20 will reveal that this is an impossible explanation, in fact a spiritually dangerous one, since it will keep
many from being spiritually prepared for Jesus' coming to
judge the living and the dead. We now turn to the longest
connected discourse of Christ recorded by Mark. It is also
recorded with additional details in Matthew 24 and 25, and
in Luke 21:5-35.

Signs of the End of the Age
Prophecy of the Destruction of the Temple

13 As he was leaving the temple, one of his disciples said to
him, "Look, Teacher! What massive stones! What magnif-
icent bulidings!"

²"Do you see all these great buildings?" replied Jesus. "Not one
stone here will be left on another; every one will be thrown down."
(Matthew 24:1,2; Luke 21:5,6)

The remark by one of his disciples, as Jesus left the temple
for the last time, was a natural one. We too are impressed
when we view beautiful churches and monumental buildings.
The temple in Jerusalem was perhaps more spectacular than
anything we have ever seen. Herod the Great started rebuilding it about 20 B.C. The rebuilding, which included the court-
yards and the surrounding walls, was still in progress at this
time. The stones were massive. Some of them, as Josephus
the ancient historian tells us, were 40 feet by 12 feet by 8 feet.
Nor was the temple just one building, but a complex of
buildings. The disciples thought that here surely was something built to stand as long as this world would stand.

They were mistaken. When those governing the temple rejected the word of God and rejected the authority of his Son, Jesus Christ (see 11:27-33; 12:12,38-40), they wrote their own ticket of destruction (see Matthew 23:37-39). It would be only a matter of time.

In A.D. 70 the Roman army fulfilled these words of Jesus by completely destroying the temple buildings. Even their exact location on the temple mount can no longer be determined. And, as though to demonstrate that he had rejected the temple, God has since permitted the Moslems to build their Dome of the Rock on that very site. Part of the great retaining wall still stands, but that was not part of the temple itself. Even its use today as the Wailing Wall does not turn hearts to the one and only Savior, the Lord Jesus Christ. Israel's history shows that Jesus came to his own and his own did not receive him. May we never make the same fatal mistake!

The Disciples' Twofold Question

³As Jesus was sitting on the Mount of Olives opposite the temple, Peter, James, John and Andrew asked him privately, ⁴"Tell us, when will these things happen? And what will be the sign that they are all about to be fulfilled?"
(Matthew 24:3; Luke 21:7)

It seems that it was in shocked silence that the disciples followed Jesus to the Mount of Olives. There they had a full view of the temple compound in all its glory. It was then that four disciples, the first ones chosen by Jesus (1:16-20), asked him a question to which all of them desired an answer. These four also had all been disciples of John the Baptist who had spoken of the end of all things (see Matthew 3:12).

Andrew was here added to the members of the inner circle, perhaps because it was Andrew who put the question to

Jesus. He and John were the first of the Twelve to become followers of Jesus three years before (see John 1:35-39). After that Andrew went to find his brother Peter and told him, "We have found the Messiah." His question here indicated that he still believed this with all his heart. He believed Jesus had the answer.

"These things" included the destruction of the temple of which Jesus had just spoken and, according to Matthew 24:3, "the sign of your coming and of the end of the age."The four disciples believed that Jesus would indeed come again. They also believed that there would be an end of the age. They were sincere and not just nosy when they asked, "When?" and "What will be the sign?" Jesus answered accordingly. He did not reveal the date to them, for that would have been spiritually dangerous. But he did speak in detail of the signs and of what would happen in the meantime. Thus he prepared them and us for the trials they, and we as well, would have to face.

Warnings Against Deceivers and False Signs of the End

5Jesus said to them: "Watch out that no one deceives you. 6Many will come in my name, claiming, 'I am he,' and will deceive many. 7When you hear of wars and rumors of wars, do not be alarmed. Such things must happen, but the end is still to come. 8Nation will rise against nation, and kingdom against kingdom. There will be earthquakes in various places, and famines. These are the beginning of birth pains.
(Matthew 24:4-8; Luke 21:8-11)

These words of Jesus read like a page out of our daily newspaper: cults with their messiahs, wars and threats of war, nations warring against nations, earthquakes and famines. We have them all. They are the evidence that sin has corrupted all things and that only the Lord's coming can finally set things straight. Perhaps the situation is even more critical in our day than in Jesus' day, for at that time Rome had enforced a relative peace on the entire civilized world. Jesus clearly states it would not remain that way, and it hasn't.

Jesus' words have been fulfilled again and again, even the first sign — false messiahs. They appeared before the destruction of Jerusalem, and there have been any number since. They are among us now. One especially comes to mind: Rev. Sun Myung Moon in 1982 in a federal court testified that he had met Moses, Buddha and Jesus Christ and that Jesus Christ had "requested me to help him in the salvation of the universe." Moon said that although he did not call himself the Messiah, his followers believed in him, and then added, "I have the possibility of becoming the real Messiah." Need we say more? Christ told us, "Watch out that no one deceives you." Christ is the one and only Messiah.

However Jesus does not say that all these signs are indications that the end is present, but that the end is truly coming. They are "the beginning of birth pains."Or as St. Paul later put it, "We know that the whole creation has been groaning as in the pains of childbirth right up to the present time. Not only so, but we ourselves, who have the firstfruits of the Spirit, groan inwardly as we wait eagerly for our adoption as sons, the redemption of our bodies" (Romans 8:22,23).

When Jesus says, "Such things must happen," he indicates that God has a hand in it. Even as God is fulfilling these signs now, so God will also fulfill the promise of Jesus' coming. Today, indeed, "the end is still to come," but his words, fulfilled as they have been repeatedly, assure us that the end will indeed come. The owner is away on a journey, but he will most certainly return (vv 34-37).

Warnings of Persecution and Strife, a Call to Steadfastness

⁹"You must be on your guard. You will be handed over to the local councils and flogged in the synagogues. On account of me you will stand before governors and kings as witnesses to them. ¹⁰And the gospel must first be preached to all nations. ¹¹Whenever you are arrested and brought to trial, do not worry beforehand about what to say. Just say whatever is given you at the time, for it is not you speaking, but the Holy Spirit.

¹²"Brother will betray brother to death, and a father his child. Children will rebel against their parents and have them put to death. ¹³All men will hate you because of me, but he who stands firm to the end will be saved."

(Matthew 24:9-14; Luke 21:12-19)

With these words Jesus prepared his disciples for what would face them fairly soon. What he said was not new, just more specific. In Mark 8:34 he had told them and the crowd, "If anyone would come after me, he must deny himself and take up his cross and follow me." Jesus' disciples were brought before councils and synagogues and before Gentile governors and kings. The Holy Spirit supplied them with the proper answers. Read Acts 5:40,41; 6:12—7:60; 8:1-3; 16:22-24; 24:1-23.

Jesus also told the disciples why it was necessary, namely, "the gospel must first be preached to all nations." Thus their sufferings would not be because of some shortcomings or sins on their part, but "on account of me" (v 9). Through their preaching, and the suffering that went with it, others would be brought to know the good news of Jesus Christ. That would be worth it.

Jesus did not withhold from them how painful their sufferings would be. The gospel is a divider; those who hear it are either for it or against it. And so the preaching of the gospel would pit brother against brother, father against child, children against parents. We sense the hurt when Paul in 2 Timothy 4:10 said, "Demas, because he loved this world, has deserted me." In fact, Jesus told them, "All men will hate you because of me." It is always only a few who accept the gospel testimony. The great majority rejects it and hates those who confess it.

Jesus told his disciples that on the way to the end, life as a Christian and as a spokesman for Christ would not be easy. Although these words clearly applied to the disciples who were sitting with Jesus on the Mount of Olives, they likewise apply to us. The world still has a fanatical hatred for Christ and his gospel. Even worse, a large share of this hatred has today invaded the outward church as many theologians reject what the Scriptures teach about Christ. Being a faithful, confessing Christian still subjects you to hatred and persecution, and in some countries even to death. Though it is not getting any better, Jesus doesn't want us to become discouraged. Here he promises, "He who stands firm to the end will be saved."

When will that end be? Jesus does not say specifically. Rather, he points to our assignment: "The gospel must first be preached to all nations." So instead of being concerned about the exact date, let us go forward using our time and talents to witness for him. The Holy Spirit, yes, Christ himself (see Luke 21:15), will help us face and overcome the trials. And the end spells salvation for all believers.

Signs Preceding the Destruction of Jerusalem and the Temple

14"When you see 'the abomination that causes desolation' standing where it does not belong — let the reader understand —then let those who are in Judea flee to the mountains. 15Let no one on the roof of his house go down or enter the house to take anything out. 16Let no one in the field go back to get his cloak.

¹⁷How dreadful it will be in those days for pregnant women and nursing mothers! ¹⁸Pray that this will not take place in winter, ¹⁹because those will be days of distress unequaled from the beginning, when God created the world, until now — and never to be equaled again. ²⁰If the Lord had not cut short those days, no one would survive. But for the sake of the elect, whom he has chosen, he has shortened them. ²¹At that time if anyone says to you, 'Look, here is the Christ!' or, 'Look, there he is!' do not believe it. ²²For false Christs and false prophets will appear and perform signs and miracles to deceive the elect — if that were possible. ²³So be on your guard; I have told you everything ahead of time."
(Matthew 24:15-27; Luke 21:20-24)

Jesus in this section is speaking of the destruction of Jerusalem and the temple. That he is not speaking of the end of the world is clear from the words: "Let those who are in Judea flee to the mountains." There will be no opportunity to flee when the end of the world comes, nor will it affect only Judea. His words "never to be equaled again" also indicate that there are days and years to follow these "days of distress."

Since the destruction of Jerusalem and the temple had as yet not taken place when Mark recorded these words of our Lord, he (as also Matthew) added the words, "let the reader understand." The Christians in Jerusalem and Judea —according to the Book of Acts they numbered in the thousands — should seize the opportunity to flee. Jesus here warned that there would be no time to waste, no time to go down into their homes to take along precious items, no time to go to the other side of the field to pick up a cloak. Josephus the historian tells us the Christians did indeed heed this warning and fled to Pella east of the Jordan.

The opening words of our Lord are the most difficult to understand. Just what does Jesus mean by "the abomination that causes desolation"? Matthew 24:15 tells us this is an expression used by Daniel the prophet and quoted from him by Jesus (see Daniel 9:27; 11:31; 12:11). The people of Judea in 168 B.C. had a preview of what could happen, when Antiochus IV Epiphanes set up a pagan altar in the temple. But the real fulfillment was the destruction of Jerusalem and the temple by the Romans in A.D. 70. The presence of Jewish insurgents with their weapons in the temple during the siege of Jerusalem and the Roman soldiers planting their battle standards at the eastern gate of the temple and offering pagan sacrifices there shows that the temple was desecrated by both Jews and Gentiles. Titus, the Roman general, after capturing the city and taking the temple, completely razed the temple structures. What the fire had not destroyed, the Roman soldiers did.

The fulfillment of Jesus' prophecy of the horrors of those days has been completely substantiated by the Jewish historian Josephus, who was an eyewitness. I remember reading all about it as a child when my father and I attended German services. Our German hymnal had an appendix which in part VIII contained the whole story as related by Josephus. Anyone who read that story would agree completely with what our Lord here said, "Those will be days of distress unequaled from the beginning, when God created the world, until now — and never to be equaled again." But the prayers of the elect were heard. It didn't happen in winter. The date of the Roman victory was September 8, A.D. 70. Note that here our Lord supports creation and not the theory of evolution, even as in 10:6. He should know; he was there.

In the months and years immediately before the destruction of Jerusalem, many false Christs and false prophets were active among the people. This aspect of the prophecy, as noted in the comments on verse 5 (p 182), also applies to the days between the destruction of Jerusalem and the second coming of Christ. Therefore Jesus' warning to his disciples on the Mount of Olives also applies to us: "So be on your guard; I have told you everything ahead of time." He did indeed. What happened to Jerusalem in A.D. 70 makes us sure that all the other prophecies of this chapter will also be fulfilled. But Christ's words are always fulfilled, as we learn in the chapters to come which describe his passion and fulfill all his prophecies about that.

The Coming of the Son of Man

²⁴"But in those days, following that distress, 'the sun will be darkened, and the moon will not give its light; ²⁵the stars will fall from the sky, and the heavenly bodies will be shaken.'

²⁶"At that time men will see the Son of Man coming in clouds with great power and glory. ²⁷And he will send his angels and gather his elect from the four winds, from the ends of the earth to the ends of the heavens."

(Matthew 24:29-31; Luke 21:25-28)

Our Lord is speaking here of all the suffering from the day of Pentecost to the end of the world, until the gospel has been preached to all nations (v 10). Preaching the gospel and believing it not only impart the joy of salvation to those chosen by our Lord, but are also met with opposition and hatred (v 13). This will continue until our Lord comes again, and then the end will be there. At that time the distress also will take another form, that of judgment, as in the destruction of Jerusalem.

The second coming of our Lord includes the end of the universe as we know it. Sun and moon will cease to function; stars will fall; planets will collapse. They have served their purpose, and he who made them will shake them. Another graphic picture occurs in 2 Peter 3:10. Whether this means annihilation and thus a totally new creation, or means a renovation is something Scripture does not specify.

The moment God brings history to an end is the moment when the Son of Man will come in the clouds of heaven to judge the living and the dead. Who is this Son of Man? Jesus consistently used this term to refer to himself (see 2:10,28; 9:9,12,31; 10:33; 14:21,41). He used it also in 8:38 and 14:62 when speaking of his coming in judgment as here (v 26). So the disciples knew it was the same Jesus speaking with them on the Mount of Olives, the one who would shortly suffer and die for the sins of the world, who would also come to judge the world. We therefore also know him who will preside at the final judgment.

Then he will come in glory and power and not in the state of humiliation. Although he will still have his human body, he will still be the Son of Man. He reveals his power and authority by stating that he will send his angels; he has authority over them. His unity with the Father in the Godhead is clarified or defined when he here calls the elect "his," whereas in verse 20 he spoke of the elect as chosen by the Lord.

Jesus tells us that his purpose in coming is to gather the elect to himself. That removes all fear of the judgment for us. Read 1 Thessalonians 4:16,17. No matter where we are or where our bodies or bones or dust or ashes may lie, the Lord's angels will find us and bring us to him. While verse 27 does not expressly mention the resurrection, that is certainly implied.

In this connection Mark quoted no direct words of Jesus concerning the fate of the unbelievers, because this discourse was meant to forewarn and strengthen the believers. Jesus in other words spoken by him had already indicated that the unbelievers will be given over to everlasting punishment in hell (see 3:29; 8:36,38; 9:43-48). They will no longer be present to tempt us or to persecute us. We will be with the Lord.

The Lesson of the Fig Tree

28"Now learn this lesson from the fig tree: As soon as its twigs get tender and its leaves come out, you know that summer is near. 29Even so, when you see these things happening, you know that it is near, right at the door. 30I tell you the truth, this generation will certainly not pass away until all these things have happened. 31Heaven and earth will pass away, but my words will never pass away."

(Matthew 24:32-35; Luke 21:29-33)

The lesson of the fig tree is simple. When the twigs and leaves sprout, summer is at hand. Thus, when you see the signs mentioned in this chapter, the end is near. However, we must remember that God does not look at time the way we do. "For a thousand years in your sight are like a day that has just gone by, or like a watch in the night" (Psalm 90:4). From the time the apostles took the gospel out into the world to the destruction of Jerusalem, to the growth of the church, to its persecution from within and without, to the end of all things is one chapter in God's sight, the final chapter. Jesus has a purpose in speaking this way, so that we might never say his coming is due on such and such a date and then delay getting ready.

Many have set dates for our Lord's coming and have been thoroughly embarrassed. Charles Taze Russell, the founder of the Jehovah Witnesses sect, prophesied that Christ would come visibly in 1914 to set up an earthly kingdom. When Christ did not come, he changed it to an invisible coming. But that certainly does not agree with verse 26 of this chapter. The Lord will come visibly. He hasn't told us the hour, but he wants us to be ready at all times to welcome him.

This also helps us understand the next words of Jesus: "This generation will certainly not pass away until all these things have happened." What is meant by "this generation"?

Only the people living at Jesus' time? Then we would have to admit that Jesus was guilty of an error, in fact, of affirming his error with an oath, for he began his statement with "I tell you the truth."

The Greek word translated "generation" indeed usually means those living at a given time, contemporaries. But it can also mean those descended from a common ancestor, a clan or a race. Thus the NIV in the footnote to verse 30 has "Or *race*." Many commentators have therefore taken this word to mean the Jews. Seemingly that's a viable explanation. Most people and nations living at that time have disappeared, but the Jews have not. This explanation has been misused in order to persecute the Jews, to withhold the gospel from them, to teach falsely that they do not need the gospel in order to be saved or to support Zionism and a homeland for the nation of Israel.

The explanation I prefer is that "generation" here means those who have something in common — the common denominator being rejection of Jesus Christ and hatred for those who believe in him (8:38).

For the sake of the disciples, who were often perplexed and in doubt, Jesus added a statement concerning the reliability of his word and predictions. Heaven and earth will grow old like a garment (vv 24,25) and pass away, but his words will never pass away. Many days and years may pass, but the end will most certainly come. At that moment Jesus also will come to gather all believers to himself. That's a real antidote for despair.

The Day and Hour Unknown, the Necessity of Watchfulness

32"No one knows about that day or hour, not even the angels in heaven, nor the Son, but only the Father. 33Be on guard! Be alert! You do not know when that time will come. 34It's like a man going

away: He leaves his house and puts his servants in charge, each with his assigned task, and tells the one at the door to keep watch.

35"Therefore keep watch because you do not know when the owner of the house will come back — whether in the evening, or at midnight, or when the rooster crows, or at dawn. 36If he comes suddenly, do not let him find you sleeping. 37What I say to you, I say to everyone: 'Watch!' "

(Matthew 24:36-51; Luke 21:34,35)

In his closing words Jesus once more stated how presumptuous and wrong those are who seek to predict the date when the world will end, even approximately. No one knows the date and hour, neither the disciples, nor the angels, nor the Son, only the Father. This was neither the first time nor the last that Jesus said words to a similar effect (see Matthew 20:23 and Acts 1:7).

It is the expression "nor the Son" that startles. Recall that Colossians 2:3 states that in Christ "are hidden all the treasures of wisdom and knowledge." Jesus himself says in John 10:30, "I and the Father are one." They are two persons, but one in essence; the third person is the Holy Spirit. How can Jesus then say, "Nor the Son"?

The solution — admittedly also beyond our comprehension — is that Christ here referred to himself as the Son of God who is the Son of Man. According to his human nature he laid aside the full and constant use of his divine omniscience and used it only when it became necessary for his redemptive work. It was not part of the Son's work to reveal the exact date of his second coming; in fact, to have done so would have been spiritually dangerous for us.

It is not the duty of the owner of the house to tell his servants exactly when he will return, but it is the duty of a faithful doorkeeper to be watching. The owner may return at any hour: in the evening (6:00-9:00 P.M.), at midnight

(9:00-12:00 P.M.), when the rooster crows (12:00-3:00 A.M.) or at dawn (3:00-6:00 A.M.) — the four watches of the night as the Romans reckoned them.

Christ's exhortation thus was: "Be on guard! Be alert!" Don't immerse yourself in the things of this world and thus lose your own soul. Always keep your eyes fixed on Jesus Christ. Christ's last words on the Mount of Olives, even as all of his words, are also meant for us: "What I say to you, I say to everyone: 'Watch!' "

Possibly Christ and his disciples spent that evening and Wednesday of Holy Week in Bethany.

Jesus Anointed at Bethany

14 Now the Passover and the Feast of Unleavened Bread were only two days away, and the chief priests and the teachers of the law were looking for some sly way to arrest Jesus and kill him. ²"But not during the Feast," they said, "or the people may riot."

³While he was in Bethany, reclining at the table in the home of a man known as Simon the Leper, a woman came with an alabaster jar of very expensive perfume, made of pure nard. She broke the jar and poured the perfume on his head.

⁴Some of those present were saying indignantly to one another, "Why this waste of perfume? ⁵It could have been sold for more than a year's wages and the money given to the poor." And they rebuked her harshly.

⁶"Leave her alone," said Jesus. "Why are you bothering her? She has done a beautiful thing to me. ⁷The poor you will always have with you, and you can help them any time you want. But you will not always have me. ⁸She did what she could. She poured perfume on my body beforehand to prepare for my burial. ⁹I tell you the truth, wherever the gospel is preached throughout the world, what she has done will also be told, in memory of her."

¹⁰Then Judas Iscariot, one of the Twelve, went to the chief priests to betray Jesus to them. ¹¹They were delighted to hear this

and promised to give him money. So he watched for an opportunity to hand him over.

(Matthew 26:1-16; Luke 22:1-6; John 12:1-8)

John in his Gospel places the anointing at Bethany on the evening before Palm Sunday, six days before Jesus' crucifixion and death. Both Mark and Matthew record the event during Holy Week because it reveals the attitude of the disciples and especially exposes Judas's heart. This helps us understand how it was possible for "one of the Twelve" to betray Jesus.

According to John it was primarily Judas who raised objections to Mary's deed because the proceeds would not be given to the poor (the holy excuse he used), but really because he wouldn't be able to lay his hands on at least part of what would have amounted to a year's wages. Shortly after this he contacted the high priests and agreed to betray Jesus.

John placed the account of the anointing of Jesus into its actual time setting because Lazarus, whom Jesus had raised from the dead, was also present at the feast in Simon's house. His presence attracted many who were curious and many who because of Lazarus had come to faith in Jesus (see John 12:9-11). It was this faith-attraction to Jesus which the high priests feared above all else. Since neither Mark nor Matthew date the event, there is no contradiction between them and John.

Two days before the Passover and the Feast of Unleavened Bread the Sanhedrin held an informal meeting in the palace of Caiaphas the high priest (see Matthew 26:3). The subject was what to do about Jesus, and when. It wasn't the first time they had consulted concerning Christ. In fact, now they even spoke of killing Lazarus. They were convinced that putting Jesus to death was the only solution, but "not during the Feast" lest there be a riot. History reports that during the Passover celebration the population of Jerusalem at least doubled in size. Since many of those coming to Jerusalem at this time would be from Galilee and thus possibly followers of Jesus, the chief priests recognized that to kill Jesus at this time would be dangerous for them. Besides, the Romans always put extra troops on the alert during the Passover. So: "not during the Feast." But they reckoned without God. Since Christ was "our Passover lamb" (see 1 Corinthians 5:7), his sacrifice for our sins would be brought on the Passover, even though the chief priests and teachers of the law had decided otherwise.

At the dinner given in Bethany in honor of Christ, Mary the sister of Lazarus and Martha honored Christ in a very special way. She had undoubtedly heard from the disciples what Jesus had told them about his impending death. With the premonition that she would not have an opportunity to show her reverence for him or to assist at his burial, she decided to show him her respect while she still had time. The perfume she used, an import from India, was very expensive, worth more than a year's wages. Mark and Matthew record that she anointed Jesus' head, and John, who has many details not given by the other Evangelists, relates that she also poured perfume on his feet and then dried them with her hair. Jesus himself (v 8) said, "She poured perfume on my body." Mary humbled herself deeply before Christ and all those present; thus she expressed her faith.

Some of the disciples (see Matthew 26:8) — their spokesman this time was Judas (see John 12:4,5) — were shocked at what they considered a waste. After all, there were any number of poor who could have benefited from the proceeds of the sale of this perfume. Are we shocked by the hardness of heart exhibited by the disciples in rebuking Mary and in misunderstanding her action?

Jesus defended and commended her. He said that there is a time and place for everything, also a time to help the poor. But since he would not be with them very long, this was the time for Mary to confess her faith openly. He called her action "a beautiful thing." He had read her heart and knew that she had done it, as he said, "to prepare for my burial." None of the disciples were present for his burial. There were only the two believing members of the Sanhedrin who had come out into the open, Nicodemus and Joseph of Arimathea, and a few women. No wonder Jesus said that her deed of faith and love would be remembered wherever the gospel would be preached in all the world.

The severity of Jesus' words also shows that he had read Judas's heart, though the other disciples, as we see on Maundy Thursday evening, had not suspected Judas. Rebuked by the Lord, but not repentant, Judas consulted the chief priests shortly before the Passover in order to betray Jesus to them. Finding a traitor in the very ranks of the Twelve overjoyed them. Seemingly they then promptly forgot about their former restriction, "not on the Feast." The amount agreed on was thirty pieces of silver, a paltry sum (see Exodus 21:32; Zechariah 11:12). How terrifying when sin and Satan (see Luke 22:3; John 13:27) take over!

Judas was not the last of the traitors. Through the ages there have been many who have betrayed their Lord, and thus have no longer walked with him. Let up pray never to be of their number!

Maundy Thursday
The Lord's Supper

12On the first day of the Feast of Unleavened Bread, when it was customary to sacrifice the Passover lamb, Jesus' disciples asked him, "Where do you want us to go and make preparations for you to eat the Passover?"

The Lord's Supper

¹³So he sent two of his disciples, telling them, "Go into the city, and a man carrying a jar of water will meet you. Follow him. ¹⁴Say to the owner of the house he enters, 'The Teacher asks: Where is my guest room, where I may eat the Passover with my disciples?' ¹⁵He will show you a large upper room, furnished and ready. Make preparations for us there."

¹⁶The disciples left, went into the city and found things just as Jesus had told them. So they prepared the Passover.

¹⁷When evening came, Jesus arrived with the Twelve. ¹⁸While they were reclining at the table eating, he said, "I tell you the truth, one of you will betray me — one who is eating with me."

¹⁹They were saddened, and one by one they said to him, "Surely not I?"

²⁰"It is one of the Twelve," he replied, "one who dips bread into the bowl with me. ²¹The Son of Man will go just as it is written about him. But woe to that man who betrays the Son of Man! It would be better for him if he had not been born."

²²While they were eating, Jesus took bread, gave thanks and broke it, and gave it to his disciples, saying, "Take it; this is my body."

²³Then he took the cup, gave thanks and offered it to them, and they all drank from it.

²⁴"This is my blood of the covenant, which is poured out for many," he said to them. ²⁵"I tell you the truth, I will not drink again of the fruit of the vine until that day when I drink it anew in the kingdom of God."

²⁶When they had sung a hymn, they went out to the Mount of Olives.

(Matthew 26:17-30; Luke 22:7-23;
John 13:1,2,18-30; 1 Corinthians 11:23-26)

It was Thursday of Holy Week. Tomorrow, on the Passover, "Christ, our Passover lamb" would be sacrificed (1 Corinthians 5:7). Friday according to Hebrew reckoning began on Thursday evening at 6:00 P.M.

For a period of eight days, from the day before the Passover week, the Jews ate only unleavened bread to remind them of what the children of Israel had eaten on their journey through the wilderness. This eight-day period was called the Feast of Unleavened Bread. The Passover itself commemorated the eating of the lamb in Egypt whose blood had been painted on the door posts, so that the angel of death would pass over the houses of God's people. This was the most sacred season of the year for the Old Testament church. It pointed forward to the coming of the Messiah, who would save them from the bondage of sin.

On Thursday morning while still with Jesus in Bethany, the disciples asked him where he would celebrate the Passover meal. His answer reminds us of the directions he gave on Palm Sunday for finding the colt — explicit instructions, but no revelation of the exact location. The man whom the two disciples were to look for and follow would be easily identified. He would be carrying a water jar, what in that day usually was done by women. The message Jesus sent to the owner of the home reveals that this man must have been a devoted follower of Christ. He would know who "the Teacher" was, and undoubtedly recognize those who were sent. There is no hint at all of a previous arrangement, yet we cannot totally rule that out. Rooms were at a premium with the heavy influx of pilgrims to Jerusalem.

But why the secrecy? Because Jesus knew what Judas was up to (vv 10,11) and wanted to make certain that he would still have this opportunity to eat the Passover with his disciples. Besides, it would also permit him to warn Judas.

Peter and John (see Luke 22:8) went to Jerusalem, found all things as Jesus had told them, and prepared everything needed for the Passover — the lamb, the bitter herbs, the unleavened bread, the wine. When evening came, Jesus was with the Twelve in the upper room. "The Twelve" is often used as a technical term for the apostles as in 1 Corinthians 15:5, where the Twelve are really only the Eleven (see Matthew 28:16; Luke 24:9; Mark 16:14; Acts 2:14), since Judas was already dead. It is possible, of course, that Peter and John may also have returned to Jesus and that the Twelve then went as a group.

While they were eating the Passover, Jesus made a shocking announcement. One of those eating with him would betray him. No one suspected Judas, for all asked, "Surely not I?" Yes, said Jesus, one of the Twelve, one dipping bread into the bowl with him. John 13:18 states that Jesus here fulfilled Psalm 41:9, "Even my close friend, whom I trusted, he who shared my bread, has lifted up his heel against me." Mark has that Jesus said, "The Son of Man will go just as it is written about him." And then he added a warning for Judas to heed — for all of us to heed! Though Scripture was being fulfilled, that did not excuse Judas. God would hold him responsible for his actions. Judas at that moment could have refused the sop Jesus handed him and could have repented, but he did not. Instead Satan found room in his heart, and Judas left the room filled with rage and a determination to betray Jesus into the hands of the chief priests. We next meet him when he identified Jesus with a kiss in the Garden of Gethsemane. Reading this account cannot but sober us in our relationship with Christ and Christ's own! What grief this meant for our Lord Jesus! This too was part of his passion.

After Judas absented himself, Jesus concluded the Passover meal in a way which was totally new. The reason — the Old Testament Passover meal, which pointed to Christ and his sacrifice, would be fulfilled and have served its purpose when Jesus died the next day. Taking the bread and the wine of the Passover, Jesus now instituted the New Testament sacrament of the Lord's Supper.

The sacrament of Jesus' body and blood was meant not only for the Twelve (now the Eleven). Note that Jesus said, "This is my blood of the covenant which is poured out for many" — many as compared with the Eleven, and thus meant for all believers. Already three years before John the Baptist had pointed to Christ, saying, "Look, the Lamb of God, who takes away the sin of the world!" (John 1:29). When Jesus here spoke of not drinking again of the fruit of the vine until the coming of the kingdom of God, it is clear that he meant this sacrament not only for those present that first Maundy Thursday, but that it would be valid until we too would meet him again, thus throughout the New Testament age. Instead of the lamb in the Passover, Christ in this sacrament in, with and under the bread gives us his body — crucified the next day — and in, with and under the wine his blood, which would be poured out as a sacrifice for the forgiveness of our sins on Good Friday.

Perhaps no other words of our Lord have received as varied and contradictory interpretations as these. The majority of Protestants consider the bread and wine as no more than symbols of something those who partake of the sacrament receive spiritually. The Romanists teach transubstantiation, that the bread and wine are changed into Christ's body and blood, so that no bread and wine remain, only the forms. Besides, they also teach that this sacrament actually is a sacrifice being brought by the priest, the officiant. But both of these interpretations totally disagree with Scripture: "Therefore, whoever eats the bread or drinks the cup of the Lord in an unworthy manner will be guilty of sinning against the body and blood of the Lord" (1 Corinthians 11:27). There St. Paul by inspiration says that in partaking of this sacrament we eat bread and drink wine, but at the same time receive the body and blood of the Lord.

Luther is scripturally correct when in his *Small Catechism* he answers the question, "What is the sacrament of Holy Communion?" by saying, "It is the true body and blood of our Lord Jesus Christ together with the bread and wine, instituted by Christ for us Christians to eat and to drink." And when he asks, "What blessing do we receive through this eating and drinking?" he states, "That is shown us by these words, 'Given and poured out for you for the forgiveness of sins.' " And Jesus himself said, "This is my body" and "This is my blood." How is this possible? Because Christ said so. It remains a mystery, but each of us can truly say that he died for me, he shed his blood for me, and he assures me of it by in his grace giving me his true body and blood in, with and under the bread and wine of his Holy Supper.

We can be very grateful our Lord did not restrict the sacrament just to the Eleven. We are unable to save ourselves. The sacrament, however, reassures us of the truth: "Since we have now been justified by his blood, how much more shall we be saved from God's wrath through him!" (Romans 5:9). We need that assurance repeatedly until Jesus comes again to take us to the marriage supper of the Lamb. That assurance he brings us through word and sacrament. Even as we were born into the kingdom by the rebirth of baptism, so we are assured of forgiveness and strengthened to live in the kingdom through this blessed sacrament of his body and blood. Judas was excluded because he refused to repent of the sin he planned. May we daily repent and repeatedly receive the assurance of pardon as we partake of our Lord's body and blood.

As we receive it, we too have reason to sing thanksgiving and praise even as the disciples joined Jesus in singing the final hymn on the way to the Mount of Olives. "Give thanks to the Lord, for he is good; his love endures forever" (Psalm 118:1).

Jesus Predicts Peter's Denial

²⁷"You will all fall away," Jesus told them, "for it is written: 'I will strike the shepherd, and the sheep will be scattered.' ²⁸But after I have risen, I will go ahead of you into Galilee."

²⁹Peter declared, "Even if all fall away, I will not."

³⁰"I tell you the truth," Jesus answered, "today — yes, tonight — before the rooster crows twice you yourself will disown me three times."

³¹But Peter insisted emphatically, "Even if I have to die with you, I will never disown you." And all the others said the same.

(Matthew 26:31-35; Luke 22:31-34; John 13:31-38)

On the way to Gethsemane Jesus made another shocking announcement that the rest of the disciples would also desert their Lord. He quoted Zechariah 13:7 and said that when the heavenly Father would sacrifice him who alone could say of himself, "I am the good shepherd" (John 10:14), the sheep would be scattered. And that's exactly what happened (v 50).

Even before they could respond, the Good Shepherd had a word of consolation for them. He told them that when he had risen — though he would most certainly be put to death, he would not remain dead — he would meet them in Galilee for a happy reunion. Even though Christ after his resurrection first appeared to them in Jerusalem, it was in Galilee where he spent the most time with them before his ascension. It was an assurance they needed, something to cling to during the dark days to come, although they did not do so. Thus we are permitted to see our Lord's loving concern for his own, even as he faced death. Will he love us less?

It was all too much for Peter. He promptly said that although all the others would desert Jesus, he certainly would not. Clearly he for the moment did not remember the special rebuke Christ had given him (8:32,33), nor the specific warning the Lord had voiced in the upper room (see Luke 22:31-34; John 13:38). So Jesus repeated what he had already told him. Before dawn Peter would deny him not only once, not only twice, but three times. (The crowings of the rooster took place after 3:00 A.M. and at dawn.) Jesus called attention to the crowing of the rooster because Peter would hear it and thus be reminded of what he had just done, as Jesus had foretold. But Peter again rejected Jesus' word. He certainly would never deny Jesus, not even if he had to die with him. Peter did not know how weak he was.

But Peter was not alone in disagreeing with his Lord and in asserting his faithfulness and strength. "All the others said the same." And all of them were wrong. Christ Jesus had to walk the way of the cross all alone. He was, in fact, the only one who could. We can in no way contribute to redeeming ourselves.

If the Eleven including Peter, who had been with Jesus for almost three years and had witnessed his miracles and experienced the truthfulness of his words, would fail Jesus in the hour of danger, what about us? Our only source of strength is Jesus. He is ours in word and sacrament.

Gethsemane

32They went to a place called Gethsemane, and Jesus said to his disciples, "Sit here while I pray." 33He took Peter, James and John along with him, and he began to be deeply distressed and troubled. 34"My soul is overwhelmed with sorrow to the point of death," he said to them. "Stay here and keep watch."

35Going a little farther, he fell to the ground and prayed that if possible the hour might pass from him. 36"Abba, Father," he said,

"everything is possible for you. Take this cup from me. Yet not what I will, but what you will."

37Then he returned to his disciples and found them sleeping. "Simon," he said to Peter, "are you asleep? Could you not keep watch for one hour? 38Watch and pray so that you will not fall into temptation. The spirit is willing, but the body is weak."

39Once more he went away and prayed the same thing. 40When he came back, he again found them sleeping, because their eyes were heavy. They did not know what to say to him.

41Returning the third time, he said to them, "Are you still sleeping and resting? Enough! The hour has come. Look, the Son of Man is betrayed into the hands of sinners. 42Rise! Let us go! Here comes my betrayer!"

(Matthew 26:36-46; Luke 22:39-46; John 18:1)

Never will we be able fully to understand the depth of Jesus' agony in Gethsemane. He came to this garden spot, one of his favorite hideaways, Maundy Thursday evening not to relax and enjoy himself, but to undo what man had done in another garden, the Garden of Eden. There sin had entered the world. Here the second Adam — a true human being in every sense of the word, but without sin and also the Son of God — faced the horrendous debt he had come to pay. He had spoken of this many times before, but now he was face to face with it. Would he, could he, go through with it?

Like you and me, he needed to pray to the Father in heaven. But he also needed the company and compassion of his closest human friends, his disciples. On entering the garden, he became agitated as no mere martyr could be. They who suffer and die for Christ know that they have in him a Savior ready to receive them. He, however, was the sacrificial Lamb about to bear the punishment for all sin. To the three who went farther into the garden with him he bared his feelings, "My soul is overwhelmed with sorrow to the point of death. Stay here and keep watch."

So great was his agony that he not only knelt in prayer, but fell flat on his face (see Matthew 26:39). This is a different prayer posture than most artists have painted. He pleaded with his Father as a child would, that if possible the hour might pass from him. His whole nature recoiled; the ordeal was an unspeakable one. The cup — he had mentioned it once before (10:38) — was the cup of God's wrath. Although he was ready to drink the cup, nevertheless he asked the Father if perhaps in his omniscience he knew of another way to save mankind. But Jesus was ready to submit to whatever the Father decided, even though he dreaded what faced him. Three times he poured out his soul to his Father. His sweat even became like drops of blood, and the Father sent an angel from heaven to strengthen him (see Luke 22:43,44). There was no other way. Our Lord met the test and would win the battle.

The three disciples? That was another story. Jesus asked them to watch. They promptly fell asleep — even Peter who had boasted he was ready to die with the Lord. When roused by Jesus, they were too embarrassed to come up with any excuse. And so in the midst of his own agony our Lord showed his concern for his disciples. He reminded them that their own sinful flesh (rather than the NIV "body") would not be able to overcome in the battle, so they must watch and pray. When he returned the second time, he found them asleep again, and also the third time. We can feel for them. They were fatigued, and it had been a long, puzzling day. But they had failed Christ in his hour of need. He had to agonize all alone.

Because he had been strengthened by his communion with the Father in heaven, Jesus was a changed person when he returned to the disciples the third time. He had won the battle with his own human feelings, even as he had at the very beginning of his ministry when he was tempted in the wilderness. He roused his disciples. Then he told them exactly what was about to happen and went forward to meet his betrayer.

We need to remember that all this was also part of what Christ endured for our salvation, as our substitute. We need to remind ourselves of the scene in Gethsemane more than just once a year during Lent. And we can be sure that Jesus will also answer our prayers, and help us in our anxiety as we watch and pray.

Jesus Betrayed and Arrested

[43]Just as he was speaking, Judas, one of the Twelve, appeared. With him was a crowd armed with swords and clubs, sent from the chief priests, the teachers of the law, and the elders. [44]Now the betrayer had arranged a signal with them: "The one I kiss is the man; arrest him and lead him away under guard." [45]Going at once to Jesus, Judas said, "Rabbi!" and kissed him. [46]The men seized Jesus and arrested him. [47]Then one of those standing near drew his sword and struck the servant of the high priest, cutting off his ear.

[48]"Am I leading a rebellion," said Jesus, "that you have come out with swords and clubs to capture me? [49]Every day I was with you, teaching in the temple courts, and you did not arrest me. But the Scriptures must be fulfilled." [50]Then everyone deserted him and fled.

[51]A young man, wearing nothing but a linen garment, was following Jesus. When they seized him, [52]he fled naked, leaving his garment behind.

(Matthew 26:47-56; Luke 22:47-53; John 18:2-11)

This was the last time the Twelve were together. What a tragic moment! Judas exposed himself as the traitor, and the Eleven deserted their Lord.

The Sanhedrin had sent an armed corps of temple police and Roman legionaries (see John 18:3) together with some of their own members to arrest Jesus. If there was resistance, they wanted to make it impossible for Jesus to evade them, as he had so often done before. Since it was night, Judas agreed to identify Jesus by kissing him. This was the way a disciple normally greeted his master. Perhaps Judas hoped to disguise his treachery. How evil a heart becomes when it allows Satan to take over!

Jesus, however, was fully in control. The entire force, including Judas, fell to the ground when Jesus told them he was the one for whom they had come (see John 18:6). Jesus' last word to Judas was one last plea that he might repent (see Matthew 26:50; Luke 22:48). But Judas already exposed his heart when he had simply called Jesus "Rabbi," that is, Teacher, and not Lord. The armed mob then arrested Jesus, but only after it had been fully exposed as helpless. Jesus reminded them that he had been in their midst daily in the temple courts and that they had not raised a hand to apprehend him. And even now they would not be able to do so, except that the Scripture had to be fulfilled (see Isaiah 53:12; Zechariah 13:7).

Peter tried to redeem himself by drawing his sword to defend Jesus and cutting off the ear of Malchus, a servant of the high priest (see John 18:10). But Jesus rebuked Peter and then performed a healing miracle. Grace and mercy beyond comprehension! Thereby he also protected Peter and the other ten disciples. Jesus could easily have walked through the midst of those who had come to arrest him if he had so chosen. But he was determined to redeem you and me, so he permitted himself to be arrested.

The episode with Peter and his sword, Jesus' words to Judas and the armed group, and other Bible passages (12:13-17) demonstrate how far theologians have strayed from the gospel of Jesus Christ when they support rioting, rebellion and violence as permissible because of sufferings and injustices imposed by governments or those in authority. Suppose Jesus had espoused that position, where would we be today? Where in eternity?

The final two verses (vv 51,52) are peculiar to Mark's Gospel. That has led to a great deal of speculation. Could the young man have been Mark himself? Could the upper room have been in the home of Mark's parents, where the Jerusalem church later met (see Acts 12:12)? The young man (the Greek word suggests a teenager) may have been asleep in the house where Jesus and his disciples celebrated the Passover. When he heard Jesus and the disciples leave for Gethsemane, he quickly grabbed an outer garment and followed. When the armed guards came and the Eleven fled, he stayed around. In the process he narrowly avoided being apprehended and had to flee stark naked.

However the text actually does not say all that. It's only a conjecture, although a possibility. But it does reveal the temper of the armed band and point out that Jesus had to face his passion completely alone. Even his last supporter present had to flee, even as the Eleven — including Peter —had done moments before.

The Trial Before the Sanhedrin

⁵³They took Jesus to the high priest, and all the chief priests, elders and teachers of the law came together. ⁵⁴Peter followed him at a distance, right into the courtyard of the high priest. There he sat with the guards and warmed himself at the fire.

⁵⁵The chief priests and the whole Sanhedrin were looking for evidence against Jesus so that they could put him to death, but they did not find any. ⁵⁶Many testified falsely against him, but their statements did not agree.

⁵⁷Then some stood up and gave this false testimony against him: ⁵⁸"We heard him say, 'I will destroy this man-made temple and in three days will build another, not made by man.' " ⁵⁹Yet even then their testimony did not agree.

⁶⁰Then the high priest stood up before them and asked Jesus, "Are you not going to answer? What is this testimony that these men are bringing against you?" ⁶¹But Jesus remained silent and gave no answer.

Again the high priest asked him, "Are you the Christ, the Son of the Blessed One?"

⁶²"I am," said Jesus. "And you will see the Son of Man sitting at the right hand of the Mighty One and coming on the clouds of heaven."

⁶³The high priest tore his clothes. "Why do we need any more witnesses?" he asked. ⁶⁴"You have heard the blasphemy. What do you think?"

They all condemned him as worthy of death. ⁶⁵Then some began to spit at him; they blindfolded him, struck him with their fists, and said, "Prophesy!" And the guards took him and beat him.

(Matthew 26:57-68; Luke 22:54,63-71; John 18:12-14,19-24)

Jesus was on trial. This was a religious court. We would expect Jesus to receive a fair trial. We would expect a searching of the Scriptures to elicit answers to questions such as these: Is Jesus the Christ? Is he truly holy, righteous and innocent? Is he the Son of God (as Mark says in the opening verse of his Gospel)? Let us see.

In recounting Jesus' trial Mark omits the preliminary hearing before Annas, the retired high priest (see John 18:13,14,19-23). He gives a full account of the first hearing before Caiaphas but takes only passing note of the second early morning trial (15:1). Although the Sanhedrin was the legitimate ecclesiastical court of God's people, the court on this occasion broke all of its own rules. In cases involving capital punishment two trials at least a day apart were mandatory. They also had to be held during daylight hours. This was to assure justice. However in judging Jesus the Sanhedrin set aside its own regulations in order to condemn and execute Jesus as soon as possible. Its members' hearts were filled with hatred for him and with fear of the common people. Mark here introduces Peter sitting with the guards and warming himself at a charcoal fire. This proves that the trial was conducted at night. Spring nights in Jerusalem at an elevation of 2,500 feet were very cool.

The chief priests and the Sanhedrin were not interested in giving Jesus a fair trial. They were looking for evidence against him. Even the illegality that he had been arrested and brought to trial without a charge did not stop them from proceeding. False witnesses were allowed to testify. Their testimony proved false upon cross examination. Finally, two came forward saying that Christ had stated he would tear down the temple and himself build it up again in three days. Christ had indeed said something similar to that when he cleansed the temple the first time (see John 2:19). Later (13:2) he also had spoken about the coming destruction of the temple and Jerusalem. But that had been spoken to his disciples in private. Had Judas told the chief priests? But even the testimony of these witnesses did not jibe. Therefore Jesus did not dignify their testimony with an answer.

In fear that this trial would also miscarry, as the hearing before Annas had, Caiaphas the high priest stepped in. His first words to Christ expressed surprise that Jesus did not answer and assumed that the testimony brought against Christ was valid. Unlike as earlier before Annas, Jesus now remained silent. He submitted to this injustice and thus took upon himself all the rampant injustice people in authority have inflicted upon others from the beginning.

Taken aback Caiaphas then played his trump card. Placing Christ under oath he asked him, "Are you the Christ, the Son of the Blessed One?" That indeed was the real issue. Neither Caiaphas nor his court, of course, were minded to examine that issue. They only wanted to use it to condemn

Christ. Silence on the part of Christ this time would have been tantamount to denial. Caiaphas knew that, so he thought he had a "winner" no matter how Christ would answer. But Jesus laid his life on the line and stated, "I am." The answer should have reminded Caiaphas of the time God ordered Moses to tell the Israelites, "I AM has sent me to you" (Exodus 3:14). Here under oath Jesus declared that he was indeed the Christ, the Son of the Blessed One.

Then Christ proceeded to add a warning for Caiaphas and the Sanhedrin: "You will see the Son of Man sitting at the right hand of the Mighty One and coming on the clouds of heaven." On the last day the tables would be turned. Caiaphas and the Sanhedrin would have to stand before the divine judge, Jesus Christ. For them it will be a day of terror, if they have not repented. For the believer it will be the day of redemption.

The high priest Caiaphas should have recognized the words of Jesus as promising to fulfill Psalm 110:1 and Daniel 7:13,14 (read). But he did not heed the warning. He had achieved exactly what he wanted to. Tearing his clothes he declared Jesus guilty of blasphemy, and all agreed with him. It was not Jesus who was guilty of blasphemy; it was they. There are ever so many in the outward church today who agree with those first Good Friday judges and reject Christ as the Savior and as the Son of God. May we never be found among them!

The treatment Jesus received after being condemned by the Sanhedrin was beastly, with not a trace of dignity, to say the least. And the guards followed the example of their "noble" leaders. In Isaiah 50:6 the Savior was prophesied as saying, "I offered my back to those who beat me, my cheeks to those who pulled out my beard; I did not hide my face from mocking and spitting." This started in the court of the high priests. No longer permitted to carry out the death sentence of stoning, they took out their frustration on Christ in every other possible way before turning him over to Pilate.

Peter witnessed the horror and later wrote: "He committed no sin, and no deceit was found in his mouth. When they hurled their insults at him, he did not retaliate; when he suffered, he made no threats" (1 Peter 2:22,23). But Peter realized what Christ had done for him and for us only after he himself repented. His own trial comes next.

Peter Disowns Jesus

⁶⁶While Peter was below in the courtyard, one of the servant girls of the high priest came by. ⁶⁷When she saw Peter warming himself, she looked closely at him.

"You also were with that Nazarene, Jesus," she said.

⁶⁸But he denied it. "I don't know or understand what you're talking about," he said, and went out into the entryway.

⁶⁹When the servant girl saw him there, she said again to those standing around, "This fellow is one of them." ⁷⁰Again he denied it.

After a little while, those standing near said to Peter, "Surely you are one of them, for you are a Galilean."

⁷¹He began to call down curses on himself, and he swore to them, "I don't know this man you're talking about."

⁷²Immediately the rooster crowed the second time. Then Peter remembered the word Jesus had spoken to him: "Before the rooster crows twice you will disown me three times." And he broke down and wept.

(Matthew 26:69-75; Luke 22:54-62; John 18:15-18,25-27)

Jesus had said, "Yes, I am."

Peter said, "No, I'm not." Indeed a tragic account, but one that would never have been recorded if Jesus had not truly been what he is, our Savior and Redeemer. He was willing to bring to repentance Peter who had fallen so deeply. And after his resurrection he even restored Peter to his position as apostle and then used him mightily in the work of God's kingdom. If Jesus was willing (and able) to do it for Peter, he is willing to do it for us!

After fleeing from the Garden of Gethsemane, Peter and John (see John 18:15ff) followed Jesus and the men who had arrested him to the palace of the high priest. John, who was known to the high priest, was even permitted to enter the courtyard, but not so Peter. It was John who talked to the girl on duty at the door and persuaded her to let Peter in. Evidently both Peter and John were deeply concerned about what was going to happen to Jesus. We are not told what John did during Jesus' trial, but we are told about Peter. Was Judas possibly nearby (see Matthew 27:3)?

Peter immediately sat down among the guards who had started a charcoal fire to warm themselves. A dangerous place this in the midst of Christ's enemies. He had barely done so when the servant girl, perhaps having second thoughts about letting him in, took a close look at Peter. In the presence of the guards she asked, "You are not one of his disciples, are you?" (John 18:17) and then continued for all to hear, "You also were with that Nazarene, Jesus." Her words clearly echoed the contempt of her superiors for Jesus. Just a few hours before, Peter had assured Jesus, "Even if I have to die with you, I will never disown you." But it took no more than the words of a servant girl to bring about his fall. Thoroughly frightened, Peter retreated to the entryway, the covered passage leading to the street, thinking he would be safe there.

It was at this point that the rooster crowed the first time. Peter, however, did not notice. But there is no safe place for a sinner. Soon a number of people accosted Peter again. Luke (22:58) indicates there was a man among them; Matthew (26:71) includes another servant girl. Mark reports the words of the girl who had accosted Peter before: "This fellow is one of them." Again Peter denied. His fear blanked out the memory of what Jesus had told him in the upper room. Anything to save his skin! John's Gospel says it was at this point that Jesus was transferred from the hearing before Annas to the hearing before Caiaphas. This made it possible for Peter to go back into the courtyard and to get lost among the crowd.

The next episode took place about an hour later according to Luke's Gospel. This gave Peter sufficient time to overhear much of what took place in Jesus' trial. The servant girls and some of the guards were not satisfied with Peter's answer. In the meantime they had been discussing Peter — a precautionary measure. Again they approached him. Among them was a relative of Malchus, whose ear Peter had cut off in the garden. He asked Peter, "Didn't I see you with him in the olive grove?" (John 18:26). And the others immediately added what they considered convincing evidence: "You are a Galilean."

Now Peter for the third time denied any connection with Jesus. He denied even knowing the man. He called Jesus a "man," whom he had previously confessed as "the Christ, the Son of the living God" (Matthew 16:16). To make it sound believable Peter called down upon himself all manner of curses and even swore an oath that he was not telling a lie. It was at this moment that the rooster crowed for the second time. Then according to St. Luke "the Lord turned and looked straight at Peter." It was then that Peter remembered.

The pain was dreadful. It would have been unbearable if at the same time he had not been assured by the Lord's look that Jesus had never stopped caring. Mocked, derided and suffering more than we can ever imagine, the Lord had turned to Peter in his hour of utmost need. In that hour Peter not only remembered the Lord's prediction of his denial, but also his promise: "But I have prayed for you, Simon, that your faith may not fail. And when you have turned back, strengthen your brothers" (Luke 22:32). This episode, so shameful to Peter, recorded in Holy Scripture is the Holy Spirit's way of using what happened to Peter to strengthen us to watch and pray and, if we fall, to return to our gracious, forgiving Lord and Savior. To make that possible our Savior suffered. But more was still to come.

Good Friday
Christ's Final Hearing Before the Sanhedrin (15:1)

15 Very early in the morning, the chief priests, with the elders, the teachers of the law and the whole Sanhedrin, reached a decision. They bound Jesus, led him away and handed him over to Pilate.

(Matthew 27:1,2; Luke 22:66—23:1)

This was the second session of the court. Now the whole Sanhedrin was present. Previous to that not all members had been able to attend. Also this time, according to Luke's Gospel, our Lord refused to answer their question whether he was the Christ. He had answered the first time, and they had refused to accept his answer.

The first session of the Sanhedrin had been conducted during the night hours, even though the law forbade that. This session was called to provide the other with an air of legality. The law and tradition required that in a case of capital punishment the two sessions of the court had to be conducted a day apart. The Roman regulation required that judgment should not be passed before sunrise. This court covered up its illegality with legal formality. It was determined to put Jesus to death, come what may.

At this morning meeting the Sanhedrin made the decision reached at the previous night meeting a formal resolution:

216

He is worthy of death. Since the charge of blasphemy was a religious one, the Sanhedrin knew that this would not hold up in Pilate's court. Only political charges would be entertained there. Consequently this gathering also gave an opportunity to decide what charges against Christ to lay before Pilate. Since the title "Messiah" had political overtones, it posed no difficulty for them to decide on the charge of high treason. That they shackled Jesus would immediately tell Pilate that they considered him a dangerous criminal. It all agreed with what Jesus had previously told his disciples: "They (the chief priests and teachers of the law) will condemn him to death and will hand him over to the Gentiles" (10:33).

The official residence of the Roman governor of Judea was Caesarea on the Mediterranean. During the Jewish holy days he, however, usually took up residence in Jerusalem in order that his presence might prevent any disorders. While in Jerusalem he usually lived in a section of Herod's palace. Pilate was procurator of Judea from A.D. 26-36.

Jesus Before Pilate

²"Are you the king of the Jews?" asked Pilate.

"Yes, it is as you say," Jesus replied.

³The chief priests accused him of many things. ⁴So again Pilate asked him, "Aren't you going to answer? See how many things they are accusing you of."

⁵But Jesus still made no reply, and Pilate was amazed.

⁶Now it was the custom at the Feast to release a prisoner whom the people requested. ⁷A man called Barabbas was in prison with the insurrectionists who had committed murder in the uprising. ⁸The crowd came up and asked Pilate to do for them what he usually did.

⁹"Do you want me to release to you the king of the Jews?" asked Pilate, ¹⁰knowing it was out of envy that the chief priests had

handed Jesus over to him. ¹¹But the chief priests stirred up the crowd to have Pilate release Barabbas instead.

¹²"What shall I do, then, with the one you call the king of the Jews?" Pilate asked them.

¹³"Crucify him!" they shouted.

¹⁴"Why? What crime has he committed?" asked Pilate.

But they shouted all the louder, "Crucify him!"

¹⁵Wanting to satisfy the crowd, Pilate released Barabbas to them. He had Jesus flogged, and handed him over to be crucified.
(Matthew 27:11-26; Luke 23:2-25; John 18:28—19:16)

The Mark account of Jesus' trial before Pilate is an abbreviated one. More details are given by the other evangelists. St. Mark's purpose is simply to show that Jesus was innocent of all charges, that his condemnation was unjust, that Pilate was an opportunist, and that Israel's leaders remained adamant in their rejection of Christ. It is the just one who must suffer for the unjust. Although Pilate, as he washed his hands before handing Jesus over to be crucified, said, "I am innocent of this man's blood" (Matthew 27:24), he was not.

When the Sanhedrin brought Jesus in fetters to Pilate, it accused him of subverting the nation, of opposing the payment of taxes to Caesar, and of claiming to be Christ, a king — all political charges. Pilate immediately zeroed in on the one he considered the most serious, that of being a king. John 18:33-38 gives a detailed account of Jesus' examination on this charge. Pilate soon discovered that the kingdom which Jesus was speaking of was "not of this world." His decision at that point was: "I find no basis for a charge against him." With his flippant remark, "What is truth?" he had, however, avoided coming to grips with Jesus' indirect invitation to enter the kingdom. How sad!

In announcing his decision to the priests Pilate learned that Jesus had come from Galilee, which was under Herod's jurisdiction. He looked upon this as an opportunity to avoid making a decision in a case that had become very uncomfortable for him. He therefore sent Jesus to Herod, who may have been in another part of the palace (see Luke 23:6-11). But Pilate's scheme did not work. Herod sent Jesus back to Pilate. In his trial before Pilate, Jesus fully answered Pilate's questions. However, when he faced his accusers outside the courtroom, he maintained a serene silence. This amazed Pilate, but it speaks volumes about Christ. It tells us that all the charges against him were false and that he was ready to suffer any and every injustice and indignity to save you and me.

At this time the crowd asked Pilate to follow his usual custom of releasing a prominent prisoner during the Passover. This crowd was quite different from the crowd that had welcomed Jesus on Palm Sunday. These were not followers of Jesus, but supporters of the chief priests. Pilate saw this as another opportunity to rid himself of this embarrassing case. He gave the crowd a choice between Barabbas, guilty of murder in an insurrection of which there is no existing record, and Jesus. There could have been no greater contrast. In fact, he suggested to them that he release Jesus. Pilate figured that the crowd would certainly choose Jesus, but he figured incorrectly. The chief priests persuaded the crowd to demand Barabbas — anyone rather than Christ!

During this phase of the trial Pilate's wife sent him a message (see Matthew 27:19) which must have disturbed him greatly. Instead of heeding the warning and setting Jesus free, he released Barabbas despite the fact that he knew all along that the chief priests had handed Jesus over out of envy, not out of loyalty to Caesar. How Pilate actually had abdicated his role as judge became clear when he asked the crowd, "What shall I do, then, with the one you call the king of the Jews?" A judge doesn't ask a question like that.

At this point Mark swiftly brings his account to a close. According to John 19:1-16, Pilate had Jesus flogged to make one final attempt to release Jesus by appealing to the crowd's sympathy. However at the demand of the mob he sentenced Jesus to be crucified. He condemned the Son of Man, who is also the Son of God, to death on the cross.

We may feel sorry for Pilate, but would we have done any better? In the trials before both the religious courts and the secular courts, Pilate was the only one who in any way defended Christ. Nevertheless he did not follow through with his conviction that Christ was innocent. Taking a stand was too dangerous politically. Yes, the Scriptures had to be fulfilled, but that does not excuse Pilate — or you — or me. The whole account paints a clear picture: a guilty world, a guiltless Savior. Thank God for him!

The Soldiers Mock Jesus

16The soldiers led Jesus away into the palace (that is, the Praetorium) and called together the whole company of soldiers. 17They put a purple robe on him, then twisted together a crown and set it on him. 18And they began to call out to him, "Hail, king of the Jews!" 19Again and again they struck him on the head with a staff and spit on him. Falling on their knees, they paid homage to him. 20And when they had mocked him, they took off the purple robe and put his own clothes on him. Then they led him out to crucify him.
(Matthew 27:27-31; John 19:1-16)

The flogging (v 15) had taken place in the presence of the mob. It was brutal to the nth degree with no limitation on the number of blows. Christ's back was torn to shreds by the leather whip tipped with metal or bone. The loss of blood was great. After that the soldiers led him back inside.

Three times previously Pilate had called Jesus king. Now he decided to let the Sanhedrin and the mob see just what kind of king he really was — certainly not one to be feared! What Mark records here is, of course, something that Jesus had previously foretold: "The Gentiles . . . will mock him and spit on him, flog him and kill him" (10:33,34). The King of kings was treated like a criminal.

All soldiers stationed in the palace were called together. Taking the purple cloak of a Roman cavalryman — undoubtedly a discard, ragged and faded — they threw it around Christ, right on the open wounds. It was to serve as his royal robe. Since a king needs a crown, they fashioned one of thorny brier branches. They placed a reed in his hand as his scepter. Laughing, hooting and shouting they knelt before him and said, "Hail, king of the Jews!" — a parody of *Ave Caesar, victor, imperator!* (Hail, Caesar, victor and emperor). Then they took a staff and again and again beat him over the head, driving the thorns deeper and deeper. Then, most disgusting, they spit on him. Insensitive! Cruel as can be!

Our Lord suffered it all without uttering a single word of complaint. Why? Because he is our Savior-King. For a picture of him in his glory read Revelation 1:12-16 and Matthew 25:31-46. On the last day Pilate and his soldiers will be standing before him, also the priests and the mob, and you and I. But we will have nothing to fear; he suffered all this for us.

Pilate made a final attempt to get off the hook by bringing Jesus crowned and robed as a mock king before the mob (see John 19:5-16), but both priests and people rejected him with the words, "We have no king but Caesar." Clothed again in his own garments, bloody by this time, Jesus was led out to be crucified.

The Crucifixion

21A certain man from Cyrene, Simon, the father of Alexander and Rufus, was passing by on his way in from the country, and

The Raising of the Cross

they forced him to carry the cross. ²²They brought Jesus to the place called Golgotha (which means The Place of the Skull). ²³Then they offered him wine mixed with myrrh, but he did not take it. ²⁴And they crucified him. Dividing up his clothes, they cast lots to see what each would get.

²⁵It was the third hour when they crucified him. ²⁶The written notice of the charge against him read: THE KING OF THE JEWS. ²⁷They crucified two robbers with him, one on his right and one on his left. ²⁹Those who passed by hurled insults at him, shaking their heads and saying, "So! You who are going to destroy the temple and build it in three days, ³⁰come down from the cross and save yourself!"

³¹In the same way the chief priests and the teachers of the law mocked him among themselves. "He saved others," they said, "but he can't save himself! ³²Let this Christ, this King of Israel, come down now from the cross, that we may see and believe." Those crucified with him also heaped insults on him.

(Matthew 27:32-44; Luke 23:26-43; John 19:17-24)

All the Evangelists except John tell us about Simon being drafted to carry Jesus' cross when it became too much for our Lord. Jesus' weakness should not surprise us. Consider the spiritual distress he had been subjected to, the flogging he had endured, and not a bit of food since the Passover meal.

Simon did not volunteer as the crossbearer, and yet what happened was a blessing. That Mark named him and his sons suggests that they became followers of Christ and were well-known in the Christian community. Just think, to be able to say, "I" — or "Our father" — "helped the Savior carry his cross to Calvary." Later the family was probably in Rome and known to the Apostle Paul (see Romans 16:13).

Simon was from Cyrene, an important city of Libya in North Africa. In other words, there were present at Jesus' crucifixion people from three continents — Europe, Asia and Africa. It reminds us of the risen Savior's later command to his apostles to take the gospel out into all the world and of what happened on the first Pentecost (see Acts 2:5-11). And not only men were there on Calvary, but also some women (see John 19:25-27; Mark 15:40,41).

Arriving at Golgotha outside the city walls, the soldiers offered Jesus wine mixed with myrrh, a narcotic. After tasting it, he chose not to drink it. He determined to face his suffering for you and me with his senses unclouded. Thus he paid the full price. One cannot pray properly or speak clearly if one is drugged, and Jesus had a task to perform. In fact, he was the only one who could carry it out. The pain would be excruciating, but he was ready to bear it.

At 9:00 A.M. the soldiers crucified Jesus. None of the Evangelists describe the act of crucifixion. To crucify the Son of God was almost unthinkable. His suffering included a great deal more than nails driven through his hands and feet, the heat of the burning sun, a raging thirst — physical pain. He was bearing the wrath of the holy God, his own heavenly Father, against all the sins committed from Adam's day to that of the last human being to be born into this world. Each sin merited eternal damnation. That's why he hung on the cross, naked, fully exposed to the taunts of men and the wrath of God for hour after hour.

The specific charge was still the same: "The king of the Jews." The members of the Sanhedrin rejected that charge as false. Pilate looked upon it as his last revenge. We accept it as gospel truth. The various wordings in the Gospels need not trouble us. According to John 19:20 the superscription was written in Aramaic, Latin and Greek, thus accounting for variations.

Christ's enemies wasted no time making his last hours as miserable as possible. The people passing by, the chief priests and the teachers of the law, those crucified with him and, according to Luke 23:36, also the soldiers heaped insult after insult upon him. Yes, only if he were to come down from the cross would they believe in him. Otherwise they would continue to consider him a fake. We know he had the physical power to come down from that cross. Remember, he had more than twelve legions of angels at his beck and call! But morally and spiritually it was impossible. He had come to take our place, to lay down his life as payment for our sins. It was this very purpose of our Lord that all these people ridiculed on that first Good Friday. We pray that many of them were later moved to repent, even as one of the robbers did that afternoon.

Many Old Testament prophecies were fulfilled on the first Good Friday: "They have pierced my hands and my feet" (Psalm 22:16); "They divide my garments among them and cast lots for my clothing" (Psalm 22:18); "The insults of those who insult you fall on me" (Psalm 69:9); and all of Isaiah, chapter 53.

The Death of Jesus

33At the sixth hour darkness came over the whole land until the ninth hour. 34And at the ninth hour Jesus cried out in a loud voice, *"Eloi, Eloi, lama sabachthani?"* — which means, "My God, my God, why have you forsaken me?"

35When some of those standing near heard this, they said, "Listen, he's calling Elijah."

36One man ran, filled a sponge with wine vinegar, put it on a stick, and offered it to Jesus to drink. "Now leave him alone. Let's see if Elijah comes to take him down," he said.

37With a loud cry, Jesus breathed his last.

38The curtain of the temple was torn in two from top to bottom. 39And when the centurion, who stood there in front of Jesus, heard his cry and saw how he died, he said, "Surely this man was the Son of God!"

⁴⁰**Some women were watching from a distance. Among them were Mary Magdalene, Mary the mother of James the younger and of Joses, and Salome. ⁴¹In Galilee these women had followed him and cared for his needs. Many other women who had come up with him to Jerusalem were also there.**

(Matthew 27:45-56; Luke 23:44-49; John 19:28-37)

The chief priests and the teachers of the law had mocked Jesus and demanded a sign, "Come down now from the cross, that we may see and believe." God gave them a different sign, in fact a number of signs, all of which were unmistakable.

The first was the darkness from noon until 3:00 P.M. "The sun stopped shining" (Luke 23:45). This darkness was the result neither of an eclipse (impossible at the time of the full moon) nor of storm clouds. It was something supernatural, an act of God. The Creator has that ability. Remember the darkness over Egypt (see Exodus 10:21-23) and the sun standing still in Joshua's day (see Joshua 10:12-14). It is uncertain whether this Good Friday darkness covered the entire earth. The KJV translates the Greek word as "earth" in Luke 23:44 and as "land" here in Mark, in referring to the land of Israel. The NIV translates "land" in both places. Could the Lord control the sun so as to bring darkness in only one portion of the world at a time? Study again Exodus 10:21-23, where the Egyptians were in total darkness, but not the Israelites, although the sun is not mentioned.

Darkness is related to judgment in Scripture (see Amos 8:9,10; Isaiah 13:9-11; Joel 2:30,31). Here it is a sign of God's judgment upon sin, both God's reaction to the judicial murder of his Son, and God's dreadful judgment upon sin as suffered by his Son. Hanging on the cross, Jesus experienced the agony of hell, separation from his heavenly Father. It was not for his own sins he suffered; he had none, but for our sins. He had become sin for us (see 2 Corinthians 5:21) and a curse for us (see Galatians 3:13). The Father in righteous wrath turned away from the sin-bearer, his Son. Although we will never be able to comprehend this, the close communion between the Father and the Son was suspended so that Christ might pay the price for our sins. The horror of it called forth from Jesus' lips the words of Psalm 22:1: "My God, my God, why have you forsaken me?" It was almost more than even Jesus could bear, and yet he called his Father "my God." He had not turned away from the Father.

From the terror and horror of these words of Jesus we now turn to the mockery of those who surrounded him. They were not minded to make his suffering any easier for him, only harder. Making a pun on the Aramaic word "*eloi*," they mockingly said, "He's calling Elijah." They had a tradition that Elijah would come before the appearance of the Messiah and would also help the Messiah establish his kingdom. Since Christ had openly confessed himself as the Messiah, their wretched mockery implied: "If you think Elijah will come for someone such as you, think again!" When Jesus at that time cried out, "I thirst," one of those present did take pity on him and offered him a drink of wine vinegar. But then the man added, "Now leave him alone. Let's see if Elijah comes to take him down." Others joined him in saying the same thing, according to Matthew's Gospel.

They did not have long to wait. Elijah did not come. Jesus with a loud cry — undoubtedly his words of victory, "It is finished!" (John 19:30) — breathed his last with the prayer, "Father, into your hands I commit my spirit" (Luke 23:46). He had completed the task his Father had assigned to him. He had paid for the sins of the world.

At the very moment Jesus died (see Matthew 27:51), the curtain of the temple, which separated the Most Holy Place from the Holy Place, was torn in two from the top to the bottom by God. With that God indicated that the Old Testament offerings which pointed forward to Christ had served their purpose. The Son of God had entered the Most Holy Place in heaven and had presented to his Father the complete ransom price. The way to God was now open for all. No longer was there a need for the high priest to enter the Most Holy Place of the earthly temple in Jerusalem once a year with the blood of atonement.

The hour was 3:00 P.M., and the priests were busy in the temple with the evening sacrifices. What happened must have caused consternation and could not be kept a secret. Mark and Matthew recorded it in their Gospels. It had become a matter of general knowledge. We see this as evidence that the Father approved of and accepted Jesus' sacrifice.

The church of the New Testament started growing immediately. There is good reason to think that the Roman centurion beneath the cross, a most unlikely candidate, was the first convert. He had witnessed all that had taken place. He had heard all the words Jesus had spoken while on the cross, including those with which he had committed his soul into his Father's hands. The centurion could come only to one conclusion: "Surely this man was the Son of God." In Luke's Gospel he called Jesus a "righteous man." The two match perfectly. May his confession ever be ours!

Among the witnesses present at the crucifixion and death of our Lord was also a sizable group of women. Three of them had ministered to Christ and his disciples during his preaching tours throughout Galilee. Together with other followers of Christ they had come with him to Jerusalem. At the time they, of course, did not know that they would witness the Lord's death. At this moment they also did not as yet know that they would likewise see him after his resurrection (see Matthew 28:8-10).

The Burial of Jesus

⁴²It was Preparation Day (that is, the day before the Sabbath). So as evening approached, ⁴³Joseph of Arimathea, a prominent member of the Council, who was himself waiting for the kingdom of God, went boldly to Pilate and asked for Jesus' body. ⁴⁴Pilate was surprised to hear that he was already dead. Summoning the centurion, he asked him if Jesus had already died. ⁴⁵When he learned from the centurion that it was so, he gave the body to Joseph. ⁴⁶So Joseph bought some linen cloth, took down the body, wrapped it in the linen, and placed it in a tomb cut out of rock. Then he rolled a stone against the entrance of the tomb. ⁴⁷Mary Magdalene and Mary the mother of Joses saw where he was laid.

(Matthew 27:57-61; Luke 23:50-56; John 19:38-42)

The burial of our Lord was a hurried affair, yet dignified. Since burials were not permitted on the Sabbath which began at 6:00 P.M. on Friday, and it was already past three o'clock in the afternoon, there was no time to waste.

Joseph of Arimathea, a member of the Sanhedrin, undoubtedly was present as Jesus died. Before he had been a secret believer in Jesus, now he came out in the open. In doing so he put his position on the line. Boldly he went to Pilate and requested the body of Jesus. He was really asking Pilate to make an exception, since bodies were usually released to close relatives and friends. The disciples, afraid and downcast, were in no position to take that action, perhaps didn't even think of it. Joseph wanted to spare Jesus the indignity of having his body dumped into a common grave. Thus he also unknowingly fulfilled the prophecy: "They meant to give him a grave with the wicked; but he was with the rich in his death, because he had done no wrong and no deceit was found in his mouth" (Isaiah 53:9 as translated in *Isaiah II*, Pieper-Kowalke, p 448). After Pilate had ascertained from the centurion that Jesus was indeed dead, a fact that surprised him because those crucified usually did not die so soon, he gave the body to Joseph.

Joseph quickly bought the needed linen cloth for the burial. Nicodemus (see John 19:39) brought the powdered mixture of spices, myrrh and aloes, in a large amount used for royal burials. Perhaps it was with the help of the centurion that they removed Jesus' body from the cross. Whether they first washed the body (the usual custom) we are not told. They wrapped Jesus' body in the linen together with the spices and then placed it in the grave. It was Joseph's own tomb (see Matthew 27:58,60). It had never been used, and it was near the place where Jesus had been crucified (see John 19:41,42). Among those witnessing the burial were Mary Magdalene and Mary, the mother of Joses, and women who had come with Jesus from Galilee (see Luke 23:55).

There is no doubt Jesus was dead. Only dead bodies receive burial. You and I know that he did not remain dead. He rose from the grave in victory. But for those who did him the last honors, that still lay in the future. At this time only sorrow filled their hearts.

The Resurrection and Ascension of Jesus
The Resurrection

16 **When the Sabbath was over, Mary Magdalene, Mary the mother of James, and Salome bought spices so that they might go to anoint Jesus' body. ²Very early on the first day of the week, just after sunrise, they were on their way to the tomb ³and they asked each other, "Who will roll the stone away from the entrance of the tomb?"**

⁴But when they looked up, they saw that the stone, which was very large, had been rolled away. ⁵As they entered the tomb, they saw a young man dressed in a white robe sitting on the right side, and they were alarmed.

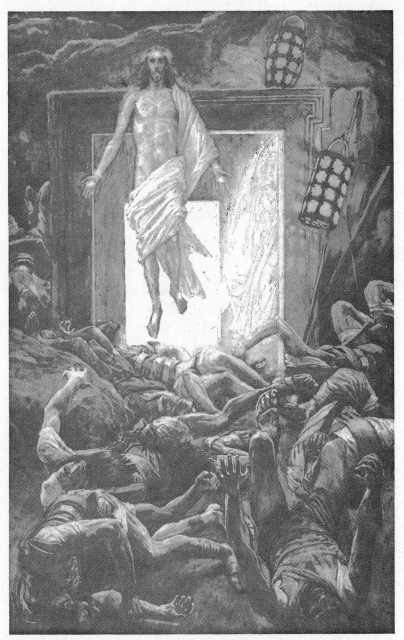

The Resurrection

⁶"Don't be alarmed," he said. "You are looking for Jesus the Nazarene, who was crucified. He has risen! He is not here. See the place where they laid him. ⁷But go, tell his disciples and Peter, 'He is going ahead of you into Galilee. There you will see him, just as he told you.' "

⁸Trembling and bewildered, the women went out and fled from the tomb. They said nothing to anyone, because they were afraid.

(Matthew 28:1-8; Luke 24:1-9; John 20:1-9)

When we read the resurrection accounts of the four Gospels, we wonder how they fit together. Many modern commentators speak of contradictions upon contradictions. If what they say were true, then the Holy Spirit would be a liar. Conservative, orthodox Lutheran scholars, R. C. Lenski and J. Ylvisaker among others, have a fine synthesis of the four accounts. We share this solution of these problems.

Early on the morning after the Sabbath Jesus rose from the dead and passed through his burial wrappings and out of the tomb without disturbing anything. To announce the resurrection the Father in heaven then sent an angel and shook the very area with an earthquake. The angel rolled the stone away from the entrance of the sepulcher to show that the tomb was empty. The guards paralyzed by fear fled from the scene.

It was then the women came and wondered who would roll the stone away from the door of the sepulcher. Seeing it lying flat on the ground, Mary Magdalene ran ahead, glanced into the tomb, and immediately ran back to town to inform the disciples. In the meantime the other women entered the tomb and were told by the angel that Jesus had risen. They were also told to go and tell his disciples, especially Peter.

Now, Mary Magdalene was returning to the tomb accompanied by Peter and John. When on the way they met the other women, Peter and John ran ahead. After viewing the empty tomb and seeing the burial linens, they returned to Jerusalem. Mary Magdalene again came to the tomb, where angels spoke to her. Then the risen Lord appeared to her first. Shortly thereafter Jesus also appeared to the other women still on their way back to Jerusalem.

Sometime late in the morning or early in the afternoon of Easter Jesus appeared to Peter, who certainly needed that assurance. Later that afternoon two disciples met Jesus on the way to Emmaus. On Easter in the evening Jesus appeared to ten apostles (Thomas was missing) when the doors were shut and locked. A week later Jesus appeared to the Eleven under the same circumstances. They had discussed everything that had happened. But it took them a long time to grasp the glorious truth of the resurrection. That is why Jesus remained among them for forty days and met with them in Galilee, away from his enemies, before returning to Bethany for the ascension.

Even when we study all four Gospel accounts and the words of 1 Corinthians 15:3-7, we know relatively little of all that happened during those forty days. That time was needed by the disciples and followers of Jesus who had experienced the terror and horror of his crucifixion, death and burial. We too have the message which they came to believe with all their hearts: "He is risen! He is risen indeed!" Now return to Mark's account.

After the close of the Sabbath at 6:00 P.M. on Saturday, the two Marys and Salome went to the market and bought spices (aromatic oils) for their last act of honor and kindness to their late Lord. They were determined to anoint his body, an action for which there had not been time on Friday afternoon. They left their homes early the next morning, and the sun was shining by the time they reached the tomb. They were unaware of the guards who had been stationed there. The only thing they were concerned about was the large rock that had been rolled in front of the door of the sepulcher. When they saw that it had been removed, Mary Magdalene ran back to tell the disciples. Salome and Mary, the mother of James, entered the tomb to investigate. They were shocked to see a young man sitting there. From his shining garment they knew that he was an angel, a messenger from God.

His message? "The one whom you are looking for, Jesus of Nazareth, is risen. He's not here. See the tomb. It's empty, and there are the wrappings." And then so that they might fully believe, they were given a special message to deliver to the disciples and especially to Peter. They were to remind the disciples of an appointment Jesus had made with them as they were leaving the upper room to go out to Gethsemane, "But after I have risen, I will go ahead of you into Galilee" (14:28). "There you will see him," the angel said, "just as he told you."

It was too marvelous to believe, and the angel's presence too awesome. They fled from the tomb. Fear filled their hearts, and as a result they didn't race into town shouting, "He's risen! He's risen!" They could hardly believe it themselves; they needed to meet with the Eleven.

We would never have heard of these women or of what happened on that Sunday if what the angel said had not been true. God's announcement is the truth: "He is risen." It is especially John who in his Gospel tells us about the meetings in Galilee. And the Apostle Paul tells us that on one occasion our risen Lord appeared to over 500 believers at one time (see 1 Corinthians 15:6).

The one whose story Mark has told us is indeed "Jesus Christ, the Son of God" (1:1). His story is the gospel, the good news.

The Closing Words

It is at this point that the reader of Mark's Gospel, who was brought up on the King James' Version, is forced to wrestle with a problem. The problem is whether these words (vv 9-20) actually were written by Mark, or not. We do not have the original manuscripts (the autographs) of the Evangelists. At best we have copies of copies. Those copies were written by hand, either copied directly or written from dictation. The latter is also true of Paul's original epistles (see 1 Corinthians 16:21; Colossians 4:18; 2 Thessalonians 3:17). When manuscripts are copied by hand or even by typewriter or word processor, mistakes can creep in. Whole verses can be accidentally omitted.

It is such an omission that has raised a question regarding the closing words of Mark's Gospel. A few manuscripts do not have verses 9 to 20. Most of today's translations call attention to this fact, among them also *An American Translation* by William F. Beck and *A New Accurate Translation of the Greek NEW TESTAMENT into simple Everyday American English* by Julian G. Anderson, both conservative Lutheran scholars.

The NIV, however, overstates the case when it says, "The most reliable early manuscripts and other ancient witnesses do not have Mark 16:9-20." Actually only two early Greek manuscripts and a few manuscripts of translations into other ancient languages omit these verses.

While the two Greek manuscripts in question, *Codex Sinaiticus* and *Codex Vaticanus*, are genuinely ancient, dating from the fourth century, they do not stand in a class by themselves as "the most reliable manuscripts." They are part of the manuscript evidence, and in this case the vast majority of manuscripts disagree with these two manuscripts and favor inclusion of verses 9 to 20.

235

It's true that in various ways some of the other manuscripts too indicate an awareness that from early times some questions were being raised about the closing verses of Mark's Gospel. But on the other hand, even the copyists of *Sinaiticus* and *Vaticanus*, which don't have these verses, may have known about verses 9 to 20 because at the place where those verses would have occurred in the manuscript, *Sinaiticus* has a blank space long enough to accomodate verses 9-20 and in *Vaticanus* there is a page missing. So even with these two manuscripts, the omission of those twelve verses is not entirely conclusive.

On balance, the manuscript evidence favors inclusion of these verses, and other objections, such as the difference in style and vocabulary, pointed to by critics can for the most part be accounted for by the change in subject matter. Hence there is really not much doubt that verses 9 to 20 were actually written by Mark.

Jesus Appears to Mary Magdalene

⁹When Jesus rose early on the first day of the week, he appeared first to Mary Magdalene, out of whom he had driven seven demons. ¹⁰She went and told those who had been with him and who were mourning and weeping. ¹¹When they heard that Jesus was alive and that she had seen him, they did not believe it.

(John 20:10-18)

This entire section is marked by brevity and compactness, typical of Mark as we have seen, for example, in 1:12,13. Unlike the Evangelists Matthew and John, Mark also does not record Jesus' longer discourses. The only time he did so was in chapter 13. This too can be taken as evidence that these words were actually written by Mark. Verse 9 tells the time when Jesus rose from the grave, "early on the first day of the week." This also suggests Mark as the author, because none of the other Evangelists mention that directly.

Jesus here appeared to Mary Magdalene. She needed this. It assured her that he who had driven seven demons out of her was indeed among the living. Now she knew that she had nothing to fear and had not misplaced her trust. She immediately went and told the disciples, thus adding her witness to that of the other women to whom Jesus had also appeared.

The disciples did not believe their words. They had to be convinced beyond the shadow of a doubt (see Thomas in John 20:24-29). We are thankful for that, for we were not present to hear the testimony of the women, nor have we seen the risen Savior. The subsequent testimony of the disciples assures us that Christ did indeed rise from the dead. They were convinced beyond the shadow of a doubt. Easter does not mean only an empty grave, but also a risen Lord.

Jesus Appears to the Emmaus Disciples

12Afterward Jesus appeared in a different form to two of them while they were walking in the country. 13These returned and reported it to the rest; but they did not believe them either.
(Luke 24:13-35)

Among those who did not believe the witness of the women were two men who later in the day set out for Emmaus. When Jesus revealed himself to them, they immediately returned to Jerusalem to tell the others. The Eleven told them that Jesus had appeared to Peter. The two told what had happened on the way to Emmaus and how they recognized Jesus when he broke the bread. It seemed unbelievable, but Jesus had risen. They had seen him.

Jesus Appears to the Eleven

14Later Jesus appeared to the Eleven as they were eating; he rebuked them for their lack of faith and their stubborn refusal to believe those who had seen him after he had risen.

(Luke 24:36-49; John 20:24-29)

The disciples deserved this rebuke. After all, those whom they refused to believe were witnesses sent by the Lord himself. How could the disciples expect others to believe them, when they in turn would be sent out to proclaim the risen Lord, if they persisted in unbelief? Besides, Jesus had even prophesied his resurrection while he was still with them.

Critics are mistaken when they say that because this rebuke by our Lord is not recorded by any of the other Evangelists, that therefore it could not have taken place and therefore also could not have been written by Mark. Each Evangelist has items which he alone records and not the others. None of the Gospels record everything that Jesus did either before or after his resurrection (see John 20:30,31; 21:25).

Commissioning the Disciples

15He said to them, "Go into all the world and preach the good news to all creation. 16Whoever believes and is baptized will be saved, but whoever does not believe will be condemned. 17And these signs will accompany those who believe: In my name they will drive out demons; they will speak in new tongues; 18they will pick up snakes with their hands; and when they drink deadly poison, it will not hurt them at all; they will place their hands on sick people, and they will get well."

(Matthew 28:18-20)

According to Matthew, all that Mark records here took place in Galilee. Thus it was a fulfillment of the angel's promise in 16:7. When the disciples, and possibly the 500 of 1 Corinthians 15, met Jesus there by appointment, he gave them this great commission.

During his ministry here on earth as he worked out mankind's salvation, Jesus' preaching and teaching was for the most part restricted to the Jews, the chosen people of God (see 7:27; Matthew 15:24). Now, however, having accomplished man's redemption, his gospel message (1:1,14) was to be preached to all people. No longer would circumcision be the entrance into the kingdom and family of God, but rather the sacrament of holy baptism (1:4). In this sacrament Jesus would bring to those baptized the mercy and grace of the gospel. But he added a warning. For those in whom faith would be lacking or who would refuse to believe, there would be no salvation. However it is not we who save ourselves by making a decision and accepting Christ. Of ourselves we can only reject Christ. It is Christ who bestows faith and salvation.

After commissioning his disciples to proclaim the gospel, Jesus also mentioned the credentials he would give them. All of them in essence were already promised in 3:15 when he called the Twelve, and also put into practice when they went out on their first preaching journey (6:13). Examples of all of them are recorded in the Book of Acts except "when they drink deadly poison, it will not hurt them at all." This, however, is on the same level with "they will pick up snakes with their hands" (see Acts 28:3-6).

The activities of today's snake-handlers, poison-drinkers and charismatics, who put all stress on these activities and in the process ignore the gospel message, demonstrate that these are no longer special gifts existing in the church today, but such as have served their purpose. The special gifts recorded in the Book of Acts are all that we need. Nowhere did Jesus say that they would continue to the end of time. What is to continue is the preaching of the gospel.

The Ascension of Our Lord

¹⁹After the Lord Jesus had spoken to them, he was taken up into heaven and he sat at the right hand of God. ²⁰Then the disciples went out and preached everywhere, and the Lord worked with them and confirmed his word by the signs that accompanied it.
(Luke 24:50-53; Acts 1:9-11)

St. Luke wrote that on the day of Jesus' ascension, the Lord and his disciples went out toward Bethany. None of the Gospels, however, tell us about the trip back to Jerusalem from Galilee. It must have been an extraordinarily joyous one. Behind them forever was the trip taken almost two months before (see 10:32-34). The Lord had accomplished all that he had come on earth to do. But on that last trip with their Lord back to Jerusalem they were reminded of all that had taken place. There on the Mount of Olives was the Garden of Gethsemane, near it the hill called Golgotha, and not far away the tomb that was empty. During the past forty days Jesus had also convinced them of his resurrection.

Now before their very eyes he ascended into heaven to sit at the right hand of the Father, as God and man to rule over all things to the glory of his Father. Here he fully answered the question he had once asked about the teachers of the law: "How is it that the teachers of the law say that the Christ is the son of David? David himself, speaking by the Holy Spirit, declared: 'The Lord said to my Lord: Sit at my right hand until I put your enemies under your feet.' David himself calls him 'Lord,' How then can he be his son?" (12:35-

37). Here was the evidence. He was not only David's son, but he was also Lord of lords.

The final words of this Gospel (v 20) are a beautiful summary statement of the activity of the Lord's apostles and messengers in the years that followed. We are still at it, and the Lord is still working through us. Are you one of his disciples? If so, are you busy doing his work? There is no better ending anyone could have written. I believe Mark did.